Surviving the Future

Arnold Toynbee

SURVIVING THE FUTURE

1971

OXFORD UNIVERSITY PRESS

NEW YORK AND LONDON

LIBRARY OF CONGRESS CATALOGUE CARD NUMBER: 77-167854

Preface

This book reproduces a dialogue between Professor Kei Wakai-zumi, of the Kyoto Sangyo University, and me. In its original form, the dialogue has been published, in Japanese, in instalments, in the *Mainichi Shimbun*. The substance of our dialogue has not been changed in the present book, but the form of it has been recast, as the form needed for a book differs from the one that is best suited for serial publication in a newspaper.

In its original form, our dialogue was a series of sixty-seven separate questions and answers. Inevitably, there were cases in which our discussion of a topic was dispersed, and there was a certain amount of repetition. The questions and answers have now been consolidated; their contents have been regrouped under headings that correspond to the principal subjects of our discussion; and repetitions have been eliminated as far as possible.

The recasting of Professor Wakaizumi's questions has been done by me, and the recasting of my answers by my wife in consultation with me. Since the answers are longer than the questions, my wife's part of the editorial work has required more time, labour, and skill than my part. My wife's editorial work has made it possible to reproduce the dialogue in its present book form, with the valuable assistance of the editorial department of the Oxford University Press, and of Miss Susan Lermon in particular. Professor Wakaizumi's enterprise and energy made it possible for him and me to record the dialogue in its original form.

The initiative for the dialogue came to me from Professor Wakaizumi whom I have known well for years, and, as soon as I had accepted it—as I did with alacrity—Professor Wakaizumi took the essential first step. He approached me with a long list of questions covering the wide range of concerns of the rising genera-tion in Japan. These questions which are grouped together, with my answers to them, under the main headings of the present book, bring out what is now in the minds of representatives of this

generation in Japan. I believe that Professor Wakaizumi's searching
questions give voice to the queries and doubts and hopes and fears
of this generation of people, not only in Japan, but all over the
World. I therefore hope that the book may be of general interest,
for members of the rising generation, and for their elders too. The
old and the middle-aged need to understand the attitudes and
reactions of the young, and they ought to be responsive to the
young's present anxiety and distress. These sore feelings have been
aroused by dire realities that are patent to people of all ages. All of
us who are now alive ought to be equally sensitive to the present
crisis in human affairs.

The members of the generation that is of student age at the
present time are the first human beings who have become citizens
of the World as a whole, besides being citizens of their respective
countries. University campuses all over the World are *en rapport*
with each other. What happens on one campus is not only known
immediately on all others; it also produces immediate world-wide
reactions. I hope that, by the time this generation has reached
my—or even my friend Kei Wakaizumi's—age, the world-
wide unity that, for present-day students, is already an accom-
plished fact, will have become a reality for people of all generations
in all walks of life, and this on all planes of human activity. The
political unification of the World is overdue now that the World
has become a potential arena for the global atomic war.

The present student generation—my grandchildren's generation—has been born to set right a time that is out of joint by
carrying through this historic revolution in the constitution of
human affairs. Your task is going to be as difficult as it is urgent,
but do not react as Hamlet did; do not resent your destiny as a
'cursèd spite'; please welcome it as a unique opportunity. No previous generation has had this opportunity, and no later generation
is likely to have it; for, if your generation is successful, the survival of mankind will have been secured, and, if you fail, you may
have no successors.

If you are to succeed, you must contrive to retain the virtues of
youth when you have reached middle age and have shouldered
the responsibilities that middle age brings with it. The virtues of

youth are disinterestedness and open-mindedness. Hold on to them. You will have twice as much need of them when you are twice as old as you are today.

Contents

Introduction

WAKAIZUMI: Professor Toynbee, you are well known as a man who has spent a long lifetime on considering the development of societies and civilizations and the meaning of human life. Today, in a period of accelerating change on a world-wide scale, humanity has many problems to face, and especially the young in every country. Questions about the meaning of life and death, peace and war, power and authority, love and sexuality in human relationships, the relevance of family institutions to contemporary life, the control and use of increased knowledge—these are questions that create great perplexity and lack of certainty.

Man is seeking in our time to reconcile the many conflicts between tradition and innovation, between religion and science, between the needs of the individual and those of society. In this quest, man will need all the help that he can receive from thinkers and teachers through all media of communication and education.

In a world in which both society and the individual personality are under threat of disintegration, education in the widest sense might help man to reintegrate his personality, to recover a standard of ethical conduct for the individual, to re-establish a harmony between the individual and his community, and to unite mankind on a world-wide scale.

In many ways the advance of science and technology has increased man's power to determine his own future. He has increased his control over his environment on this planet and he has reconnoitred an adjacent fringe of outer space. The computer not only makes possible great advances in many fields of knowledge, but, in conjunction with complex information-systems, it enables man to explore the possibilities that are open to him and to plan effectively. However, he now has the capacity either to liberate or to imprison himself. Has man become the master or the servant of this technological advancement?

It will give me very great pleasure in the next few days to put to you many of these fundamental questions. There are great current changes in ethical standards and there is the perennial problem of our human predicament. What future do you see emerging for man and for human society? In particular, I am glad that we shall be discussing the special importance today, for shaping the future, of the educational system and of the younger generation in every country.

TOYNBEE: It is evident that we shall be exploring very searching questions over a very wide area. In dealing with these questions, I am talking to anyone who cares to listen to me. But, in particular, I am thinking of young people, because it is they whom, most of all, I wish to reach. I know young people in a very concrete way, because nine of my grandchildren are now between seventeen and twenty-six years old. For me, my grandchildren stand for all people of that age in the World. They stand for the rising generation in all countries. Can we begin our dialogue? May I hear your first question?

I

The Purpose of Life

WAKAIZUMI: Science applied to technology has been producing changes in our way of life that are diverse, complex, and revolutionary. Our difficulty in dealing with these changes is being aggravated by their rapidity. A society that has been agricultural, pastoral, and rural for thousands of years is being transformed into one that is industrial and urban. The consequent confusion, pressure, and strain from which we are suffering today are moving us to reconsider the fundamental question of the meaning and aim of life. What should man live for?

TOYNBEE: The confusion, strain, pressures, complications, and rapid changes in contemporary life are having their effects all over the World, and they are particularly disturbing for the young. The young want to find their way, to understand the meaning of life, to cope with the circumstances with which they are confronted. What should man live for? This question is particularly acute for the young, but it haunts everyone at every stage of life.

I would say that man should live for loving, for understanding, and for creating. I think man should spend all his ability and all his strength on pursuing all these three aims, and he should sacrifice himself, if necessary, for the sake of achieving them. Anything worth while may demand self-sacrifice, and, if you think it worth while, you will be prepared to make the sacrifice.

I myself believe that love does have an absolute value, that it is what gives value to human life, and also to the life of some other species of mammals and birds. I can think of some birds and mammals, besides ourselves, that live for love. I also believe (I know that this cannot be demonstrated) that love, as we know it by direct experience in living creatures on this planet, is also present as a spiritual presence behind the universe. Love can and does sometimes bring out responsive love, as we know in our own human experience, and, when that happens, love spreads and expands itself. But love may also meet with hostility, and then it will call for self-sacrifice, which may seem sometimes to be in vain. All the same, love, if it is strong enough, will move us to sacrifice ourselves, even if we see no prospect that this self-sacrifice will win a victory by transforming hostility into love. The only way in which love can conquer is by changing the state of feeling, the state of mind, of some other person from hostility to an answering love. I believe, though it is hard of course for any of us to live up to this belief, that the lead given by love ought to be followed at all costs, whatever the consequences. I think that love is the only spiritual power that can overcome the self-centredness that is inherent in being alive. Love is the only thing that makes life possible, or, indeed, tolerable.

I had better say, before I go on, a few words about what I mean by love. This is so important, as I see it, that I want to make the meaning of the word love, as I use the word, clear, because, at any rate in English, this word 'love' is ambiguous. I can say 'I love whisky', or 'I love sexual relations', or 'I love chocolate'; that is not the kind of love that I mean. Or I can say 'I love my wife', or 'I love my children', or 'I love my fellow human beings', or 'I love God'. That is quite a different meaning of love, and, in some languages, different words are used for these different meanings. In the Pali language, in which the text of the Sinhalese Buddhist scriptures is written, there is a word 'tanha', which means 'craving', 'coveting', 'grasping'.

All love is desire, but there are two kinds of desire. There is a desire that takes a creature out of himself and makes him give himself to other people, to the world, and to the spiritual presence which, in my belief, lies behind the universe (I shall deal with this belief of mine later). Then there is another kind of desire which tries to exploit the universe, to draw it into the creature himself, to use it for his purposes. Both kinds are desires, but they are antithetical to each other, and we really need different words for them. The kind of love that I mean is the first kind of desire, and I am speaking about that kind of love when I speak about what man should live for.

It is true that love can turn into possessiveness and then into enmity. This is a contradiction which arises from the ambivalence of the emotion that we call 'love'. There are different kinds of love, and in this complex relation there can be antagonisms and conflict. I am not inclined to classify the different kinds of love mainly in terms of the differences between the objects of love. I should be inclined to classify by the nature of the emotion itself.

True love is an emotion which discharges itself in an activity that overcomes self-centredness by expending the self on people and on purposes beyond the self. It is an outward-going spiritual movement from the self towards the universe and towards the ultimate spiritual reality behind the universe.

There is a paradox here. This love that is a form of self-denial is the only true self-fulfilment, as has been pointed out by the founders of all the great historic religions. It is self-fulfilment because this outward-going love reintegrates the self into the ultimate spiritual reality of which the self is a kind of splinter that has been temporarily separated and alienated. The self seeks to fulfil itself, and it seeks blindly to fulfil itself by exploiting the universe. But the only way in which it can fulfil itself truly is to unite itself with the spiritual reality behind the universe, so this outgoing love, which is a form of reunion, a union with other people and with ultimate spiritual reality, is the true form of fulfilment.

I wonder whether we can, so to speak, 'harness' love; can we sublimate it, not only to a spiritual level as between men and women who have sexual relations with each other in marriage, but to levels at which sex does not enter in at all? Can we 'put love to work' for art and for action on the grand scale? Mutual love radiates out beyond the people who feel this love for each other; I think it imparts itself to everyone who comes into contact with it. Mutual love can also give inspiration and energy for achievements and creations which are ways of loving fellow human beings whom one has never met and will never meet personally. Many men and women work for people in distant times and places, just because these other people, who are perhaps not yet born, are going to be human beings like the people who are working for them in anticipation of their birth.

The privation, or the voluntary renunciation, of personal love has certainly sometimes inspired feats performed for love of all mankind, or for love of the spiritual presence behind the universe.

This is not a transmutation of love into something different from love; it is an outflow of love along a different channel and towards a different object, when we compare it with the direct interchange of love between persons. The Italian poet Dante was deprived of Beatrice, and not only of the lady he loved, but also of the city he loved, his native city of Florence. In every letter that he wrote after having been exiled, he signed himself 'Dante of Florence—undeservedly in exile'. Dante's life in exile, after Beatrice's death, was sorrowful. Yet his love, just because he was deprived of Beatrice and of Florence, gave the world the *Divina Commedia*.

The Buddha and Jesus cut themselves off from their families and they embraced mankind. Why are the bodhisattvas revered? Because they have voluntarily postponed their exit from the World into Nirvana in order to help their fellow creatures to enter this spiritual haven.

Celibacy, the renunciation by men and women of love in the form of marriage, in order to live in a community with persons of their own sex, may liberate love to embrace all mankind and to reach the spiritual presence behind the universe. Celibacy has produced some of the greatest religious achievements in history. But it may also warp human nature if it is found to be too difficult an aim to achieve. I have known a number of Christian monks who have made a success of being monks; I have heard of other monks for whom it has been too difficult. In most religious orders (I expect this is true of Buddhist as well as Christian monastic orders) there is a wise rule that makes it very easy to give up the intention of becoming a monk before you have taken your final vows. After that, it may be more difficult to obtain release, but it does happen (we hear of cases today) that a monk late in life will find his life too hard for him.

I am not sure, however, that one is truly expressing the nature of love if one talks about 'harnessing love', or 'putting love to work'. Love is not like that, not like an ox or a machine that you can put to work or can harness. Love is spontaneous activity, energy, action. You cannot distinguish love from what it does. The feeling and the action are identical.

Man is a social being, and therefore, among all the objects for his love that there are in the universe and beyond it, he ought, I suppose, to love his fellow human beings first and foremost. But he should also love all non-human living creatures, animals, and plants, as well, because they are akin to man; they too are branches of the great tree of life. This tree has a common root; we do not know where the root comes from, but we do know that we all spring from it. Man should also love inanimate nature, because this, too, is part of the universe which is mankind's habitat.

I think people in India and Eastern Asia have a greater wish, and a greater sense of the need, to love non-human living creatures, and also inanimate nature, than people in the Western world have. This wish to expand the field of human love is not so strong in the Western tradition. By Western I do not mean just Christian: I mean Christian and Jewish and Muslim, because Christianity and Islam are derivatives, offshoots, of Judaism. However, in the Western tradition, too, there are traces of this feeling for nature. For instance, Saint Francis of Assisi, one of the greatest religious figures in Western history so far, has written, in the earliest surviving piece of Italian poetry, a hymn in which he praises God for our brothers the Sun, Wind, Air, Clouds, Fire, and for our sisters the Moon, the Stars, the Waters, the Earth, and every mortal human body. Saint Francis is very conscious of this brotherhood and sisterhood of all living creatures.

There are some very difficult questions about the giving of love. The human beings and the non-human creatures that we want to love, and that we ought to love, are many, and some of them, sometimes, have conflicting interests. Ought we to love some human beings at the expense of others? It is easier to love people whom we know in the flesh, people who are alive, or who were our contemporaries but who are no longer alive. It is possible to love people whom we have never met, even people who have been long dead. I myself have a feeling, which I am sure is love, for Saint Francis of Assisi, who died about 750 years ago, and all Buddhists and all Christians have a feeling for the Buddha and for Jesus. We do not know so much about their lives as we know about Saint Francis's life, but, as far as their lives are historical and not legendary, we can love them and we do.

But then we come to non-human creatures. Is it compatible with love to use some non-human living creatures as instruments for human purposes, as slaves, like oxen or horses, or as foodstuffs which we butcher and kill to eat? Have we a moral right to exterminate those living creatures that are inimical to man and to man's domesticated animals and crops? In English, we have a word 'vermin', meaning animals that we do not want, that we think it legitimate to exterminate if we can catch them. We have another word 'weeds', meaning plants that we do not want, and that we try to root up from our fields so that they shall not take the nourishment from the crops that we wish to raise. Then poisonous snakes, scorpions, bacteria: have we obligations to them?

If you travel in India, and if you are a Westerner, you are at once struck by the fact that wild animals and birds are not afraid of you, as they are, for the most part, in the Western world. In India they are on familiar terms with human beings. This is because Indians have a reverent consideration for the life of non-human living creatures. This is particularly strong in one Indian sect, the Jains. This Indian attitude towards living creatures does give the Westerner reason to think. Is not the Western attitude to-wards non-human living creatures too possessive, too exploiting an attitude?

I have said that we should live in order to love, and I do think that love should be the first call on every human being, but I have mentioned other things to live for. One of them was understanding and another was creating. Man seems to be unique among living creatures on this planet in having consciousness and reason, and therefore having the power of making deliberate choices, and we need to use these specifically human faculties in order to direct our love right. It is so difficult to know how to apportion our love, and to decide what objects should have priority, that conscious reasoned thought is needed for this. I think, also, that using, culti-vating, and developing our human reason is all the more important because even our human nature is only very partially rational. We human beings, like non-human living creatures, are governed partly by emotions and by unconscious motives. Our human reason is only on the surface of the psyche. The subconscious depths below it are unfathomable. Our unconscious motives may be good or evil. We need to bring them up to consciousness, so far as we can, and to look at them closely, in order to see whether they are good or bad and to choose and follow the good and reject the bad. There again, we need to keep our reason and our consciousness at work. A human being's life is a constant struggle between the rational and the irrational side of human nature. We are always trying to conquer a bit more of our nature for reason from blind emotion, and we are often losing ground, and then the irrational gains on the rational. As I see it, the whole of human life is a struggle to keep the reason uppermost.

Finally, we should live for being creative. What do I mean by creative? I mean trying to change this universe in which we find ourselves placed—trying to add good things to it, if possible. The universe, in the state in which we find it when we wake up to consciousness, is obviously imperfect and unsatisfactory. Many living creatures prey on each other. All animals live either on other animals which they kill in order to eat, or on vegetation, and, apart from living creatures, inanimate nature, when it is unmodified and uncontrolled, can be extremely inimical, not only to human life, but to all kinds of life. I am thinking of the earthquakes, the floods, the droughts, the storms, and the tornadoes that may destroy hundreds of thousands of lives and wreck the works of man. This, too, is an imperfection in the universe. So we should strive to add to the universe by supplementing the natural environment in which we find ourselves and partially replacing it by a man-made environment. Here, however, we have to be cautious. Since our ancestors became human, since we awoke to consciousness, we have been working on the natural environment and changing it. We have been domesticating plants and animals, instead of gathering wild plants and hunting wild animals for food. We have been constructing buildings which are not part of the non-human natural environment; we have been building great engineering works. In the non-material spiritual side of life, we have been creating works of science and of architecture and of art which have a value for us in themselves. We do this creative work from disinterested motives, not from immediate utilitarian motives, yet this kind of work often turns out to have undesigned and unexpected practical uses.

I have now answered the question: 'What should man live for?' In my belief, love, creation, and understanding are the purposes for which man should live, for which he should give his life, and for which he should sacrifice himself if, in pursuit of these objects, sacrifice turns out to be demanded of him.

The Obstacles to Achieving Life's Purpose

WAKAIZUMI: When we find what answers we give to the fundamental question of the meaning and aim of life, are we confronted by obstacles to the achievement of the aim which is set for us by the meaning of life, as we interpret this? In face of these obstacles, attitudes diverge and ways part, making goals harder to reach. The immediately evident obstacle is the discrepancy between our ideals and the actual present facts. The rising generation feels that its parents' generation is acquiescing far too readily and complacently in the facts as they are. This attitude of their elders seems to the young to be short-sighted, cowardly, and hypocritical; for they see in it a shirking of the duty of the generation that is now in power, and they fear that this delinquency may quickly lead to a disaster which will condemn the younger generation to be deprived of the future which is every generation's birthright.

The young are indignant; their elders are resentful. Admittedly, the World is now in a parlous state, and the immediate responsibility for this lies on the shoulders of the present holders of power. Is the present mismanagement of the World's affairs due to culpable incompetence and wrong-headedness? Or are all holders of power to some extent victims of circumstance?

The insurgent rising generation is revolting against power as they see power being exercised by their elders. Can the power factor be eliminated from human relations, or is it one of the inescapable facts of social life? And, if the rebels themselves seek to exert power by resorting to violence, are they not likely to produce a 'backlash'? In the past, many attempts at revolution have been crushed by more successful repressive counter-action, and many successful revolutions have had a still more ironical sequel; in the act of succeeding they themselves have changed into repressive régimes.

The revolt against the attitude and conduct of the middle-aged generation is widespread among the younger generation, but they are revolting in two different and opposite ways. There are the militants, who are tempted by their anger, apprehension, and impatience to resort to revolutionary violence, because they see no other way of closing the shocking gap between what is and what ought to be. And then there are the 'hippies', who react to their disillusionment with society as it is, not by trying to revolutionize it, but by 'dropping out' of it. The hippies are repudiating society's traditional moral inhibitions—for instance, against taking drugs and against promiscuity in sexual relations. Are these two forms of the present revolt of the rising generation peculiar to our time, or are they only extreme manifestations of a tension between different generations that is normal?

TOYNBEE: When we probe the question of the purposes of life, we come up against a challenging contrast between our ideals and the facts. I do not think that this challenge is new in substance, but it may be new in the sense that it is much more acute for the present rising generation than for previous generations. The difference in the degree of their distress may be really equivalent to a difference in kind. It may amount to being a real new challenge.

However, when my generation in England was growing up— and I am looking back to the time when we were between, say, seventeen and twenty-six years old—we did feel the same distress, though perhaps not to the same acute degree. We were distressed by the grossly unjust and inhuman inequalities of material and spiritual conditions and opportunities as between different income-groups and different social classes in what was supposed to be the same community. In the nineteenth century, British statesmen and writers who were sensitive to the badness of these extreme social differences talked about 'the two nations', meaning the rich and the poor and implying that these were virtually separate nations in one country; or 'the two Englands', meaning England as it appeared to the rich and the very different England seen through the eyes of the poor. This is no exaggeration of the situation. I still remember how, when, as a child, I was walking to school in London, I used to be upset at seeing other little children of my own age going in rags to their school. Then, when I was just grown up, my generation in Britain was overtaken by the First World War, and we were shocked by finding that human beings were committed to this institution—war—in which it was considered not only lawful, but obligatory, to kill, wound, maim, and devastate. These are flagrantly anti-social acts, quite incompatible with love and with community and with neighbourliness. They are therefore condemned and punished as crimes and sins when committed in any other circumstances than war.

I do not think that either the present rising generation or my own generation when it was young has been peculiar in being distressed at the disparity between the real and the ideal. I think the young have felt this in every generation to some extent. I also think that in every generation the same distress has continued to be felt by people at every stage of life, in so far as they have not become resigned to the existence of the real through their experience of the difficulty of changing the real into something nearer to the ideal. I am afraid that most of us do become partially resigned, just by experience of life and by finding out how very hard it is to change the World for the better.

I myself have never become reconciled to the premature deaths of my contemporaries, on both sides of the front, in the First World War. I am distressed that they were killed in the act of trying to kill their fellow men who did kill them. I am distressed at my own share of mankind's responsibility for the existence and for the survival of the institution of war and for the outbreaks of the particular wars that have been waged in my lifetime. I am also distressed at social injustice, both within each of the rich countries and as between the rich and the poor countries. A very great majority of the human race, perhaps three-quarters of it, is still poor, below the 'poverty line', not properly fed, not properly clothed, not properly housed.

In general, I am distressed at the evil of which I am aware at first hand in myself and at second hand in my fellow human beings—the evils of selfishness, greed, callousness, and animosity; and, in feeling this distress, I believe I am sharing a feeling that has been felt by all human beings, at least at some moments in their lives, at all stages of life, at all times, and in all places.

I think that this challenge that is presented by the disparity between the real and the ideal is part of the challenge of being human. I therefore think that this challenge is as old as mankind itself. However, I think, as I have said, that it is also new, in the sense that it has become so very much more acute. But why has the challenge become much more acute? Because mankind has won for itself a greater power to change the conditions of life, to make these conditions either better or worse than they are by nature.

When our ancestors first became human, this new departure brought with it the power to change their environment. Human beings can change both their social environment (their human manners and customs and institutions) and their physical environment (the setting of non-human nature into which the human race has been born). However, during the first million years of human history, human beings were still so much at the mercy of non-human nature that we took nature, including the structure of human society, for granted. We did not yet dream that we might be able to change nature by human action.

As I see it, our distress at the disparity between the real and the ideal has increased step by step with the increase in our ability to change both human institutions and physical nature. So long as we realized that we were pretty well powerless and helpless, we did not feel this distress, because we were passive; there was nothing that we could do about the situation in which we found ourselves. With the increase in our power, our sense of responsibility and our sense of distress increases. I have said that I think that man ought to live for creating, loving, and understanding. Now to love and to understand gives us the means and the motive for creating things, but the capacity to create also saddles us with responsibility. The greater the power that we have to change the World into something nearer to our ideal, the greater becomes our distress at our failing to perform those beneficent and useful acts of creation which we know to be within our power.

Therefore I think that the challenge of the disparity between the real and the ideal has become more acute, to a degree that really does make it new, for the minority of mankind, and this is still only a minority, that has by now developed the power to change the universe. The majority—perhaps three-quarters—of the human race, in the generation that is now alive, who are still living below the 'poverty line' are almost as helpless as our earliest human ancestors. But one quarter of us are no longer helpless.

I should say that this challenge, which neither the present rising generation, nor my generation, nor our predecessors, were the first to experience, arose perhaps five thousand years ago, at the time of the rise of civilization—at a time, that is to say, when man did at last begin to have some mastery over his non-human physical environment and over the arrangement of his own social life. At that stage in his history, man's human faculties of self-consciousness and introspection led him to begin to feel the need, and the duty, of controlling himself. Unless we can control ourselves, we cannot control our relations with other people.

Power is an inescapable accompaniment of human social life. We may condemn it, but, if we overthrow the existing power-structures by revolutionary violence, we often bring on ourselves a régime that is still more tyrannical than the one that we have liquidated (I shall return to this point a little later). Every living creature is self-centred. Self-centredness is really just another name for being alive, and power is one of the consequences of self-centredness, because all living creatures are competing with each other for exploiting the universe; and this competition is a conflict of power. If all human beings could get rid completely of self-centredness, power would, I suppose, disappear. It would be non-existent if the human race consisted entirely of arhats, the Buddhist term for people who have devoted their exertions to reaching Nirvana by extinguishing self-centredness. Power would also be non-existent in a human race consisting entirely of genuine saints in the Christian sense. Of course there have been some people in the Christian world who have been listed as saints, but who have used their 'sainthood' as a means for exerting power. This is a kind of pseudo-sainthood, though probably these pseudo-saints were not conscious of their insincerity and hypocrisy.

Every unregenerate self (using Christian language), or every unextinguished self (using Buddhist language), tries to acquire power; the rival attempts conflict and the consequences are either anarchy or the imposition of overriding power, that is government. There have been situations in which there has been anarchy, though this is unusual. In Iceland, after its colonization by the Norwegians, there was a century or two of anarchy in which every individual man was really a sovereign in himself and there was no government. On the north-west frontier of what is now Western Pakistan, there was till lately anarchy of this kind. But most human societies have usually had some kind of government, which restrains the power of individuals by imposing an irresistible paramount power upon them.

I once visited a valley in West Pakistan in which every local man had once been a law to himself. Not long before my visit, one local chief had eliminated all the rest by using criminal methods. He had united the valley politically in a single state, and, as a result, the valley had obtained peace and law and order, and several hundred thousand people were much happier than they had been before. But the man who had achieved this was not happy. Probably he had acted out of personal ambition, not out of altruism. He was a very old man when I met him, and he was doing penance for his sins before he died. Here there is a puzzle. Was it a good thing or a bad thing to have committed those crimes that had produced law and order and incidentally had produced happiness for other people?

St. Francis of Assisi was a genuine saint. He started trying to lead the way of life that Christ had led according to the Gospels. St. Francis thought that perhaps he would get, at most, one or two companions; for this is a very difficult way of life to lead. To his surprise, within a few years, hundreds joined his new monastic order, the Franciscan Order of Friars, which the Pope had sanctioned. St. Francis was appalled to find himself expected to be an administrator at the head of an organization, and he resigned from the headship. He became an ordinary monk and put himself under the orders of someone else who was appointed head of the order in his place.

St. Francis's action was utterly disinterested, but the result was disconcerting, for it opened the way for a man called Brother Elias, who was not a saint at all, to take St. Francis's place. Many people from all parts of the World go to Assisi and visit the church that Brother Elias built in honour of St. Francis. It is a very beautiful church, and Brother Elias commissioned the painter Giotto to paint some beautiful frescoes of St. Francis's life inside the church. But this caused a scandal at the time, because Brother Elias, in building that church, and in asking for subscriptions for it ('fund-raising' as it is called nowadays), was negating everything for which St. Francis had stood. He was not entirely successful in this, for the present Franciscans do still have some of St. Francis's spirit.

Then there is the case of the saintly Pope Celestine V. Towards the end of the thirteenth century the Papacy had got into a very bad way; it had become very political-minded, very military-minded, and the cardinals thought: 'We must make a reform.' So they found a peasant who had become a hermit up in the mountains; they brought him out and said: 'You have to be Pope.' After four months he could not bear it and he went back to his hermitage. Like St. Francis, Pope Celestine V could not abide the task of exercising authority. To him administration meant something worldly or even criminal. But what happened? Pope Celestine V was succeeded by Pope Boniface VIII, a man who grasped at the power of the Papacy, but who was a very bad statesman. He could not calculate the balance of power, so he brought the Papacy to a great disaster. Was Pope Celestine V's abdication from the Papacy after four months right or wrong? This is a very difficult question to answer. The difficulty illustrates one of the puzzles about this problem of power.

Our only practical solution, so far, has been to control individual power by collective power. This was the way in which that local ruler on the north-west frontier of West Pakistan controlled individual power.

In the face of collective power, the individual is helpless, and, because of that, I think all forms of government, including so-called democracy, are tyrannical. I happen to live in a country that is a democracy in the sense of having a form of parliamentary government. There are many other democratic countries, and people in those countries are all aware that, democracy or not, when we meet the taxation official, or the draft board which is going to mobilize us for military service, or the police, or when we find ourselves in prison, or when the death penalty is imposed on us, if there is a death penalty in our country, we are in the hands of an extremely powerful authority against which we are virtually helpless.

A distinguished nineteenth-century historian, Lord Acton, once wrote: 'All power corrupts, and absolute power corrupts absolutely.' This dictum is very striking, and no one has been able to find the answer to it or to refute it, I think.

Government means, in the last resort, imposing the will of the rulers on their individual subjects. You may call them citizens, yet they are only subjects, because their Government coerces them, if necessary, by violence. This is what we mean by law and order.

Power is a fact of life, and it has to be exercised by some human beings over other human beings. How ought power to be exercised? I think that, for anyone who is in power, the first thing that he ought to do is to begin with himself, to realize that he too is a miserable sinner, that he is really not fit to exercise power over himself, let alone over other people. Therefore, he should not feel that his position is a privilege and a grand thing to be enjoyed; he should feel it to be a burdensome task, and, if he undertakes it, he should be conscious of the weight of it. At my school in England, the head of the school was entrusted with a great deal of power and responsibility for a boy of eighteen. On the foot of his bed, an official bed on which he kept sticks for beating other boys, there were written three Greek words. Translated into English these were: 'Rule (meaning power) will reveal the man', that is, will show what kind of a man he is. This is very true, and it is very formidable for anybody in power. It is a good motto for any ruler.

Should a man hate taking power, as St. Francis and Pope Celestine V hated it? And should he reject it, or should he bear it as a burden like the Roman philosopher emperor, Marcus Aurelius? Marcus did stay in office all his life, but he, too, found power a grievous burden; he would rather have been a private person. The Greek philosopher Plato said that the only people fit to rule were philosophers, and that they ought to be unwilling rulers if they were real philosophers.

There have been rulers who have abdicated. I can think of two famous examples. The first is the Emperor Diocletian. He had restored the Roman Empire after it had suffered a collapse, and, when he had done the job, he stepped out and left it to other people. In the sixteenth century in Western Europe, the Emperor Charles V had acquired an amazing collection of kingdoms and states, and, when he had succeeded to the throne as a young man, he had seemed to have a brilliant career in front of him. In middle age he became weary and disillusioned and he abdicated.

This is a difficult question. If a ruler does not have zest, will he exercise power well? You cannot do anything well unless you have a zest for it. Many successful administrators have had zest; for instance Nobunaga, Hideyoshi, and Ieyasu in Japan and Lenin in Russia. The first Chinese Emperor, Shih Hwangti, had zest, and so had Augustus in the Roman Empire. In medieval Europe there were Louis XI of France and Henry VII of England. I do not say that these were good men, but certainly they were effective rulers, and they were effective because they enjoyed practising the art of ruling. Yet does not zest for power corrupt, in the way that Lord Acton suggested? Did power corrupt Lenin? Perhaps not, but it certainly corrupted Stalin. It may not have corrupted Robespierre, but it certainly corrupted Napoleon.

The very nature of power tempts the holders of it to abuse it to some extent, and this provokes their subjects—especially those in the rising generation—to indict them. I do not believe that the present holders of power are 'guilty' in the sense of being uniquely corrupt and incompetent. In every society it is the middle-aged generation that is momentarily in power and that therefore bears the immediate responsibility for the current state of society. Consequently I think that the middle-aged generation should reproach itself, and not the younger generation first, when 'the time is out of joint.' Hamlet had a just grievance. For someone of his age—he was a university student—it was monstrous that his mother and his uncle should have so misbehaved that it fell to him to put things right. This duty cost him his life. It is not fair on the younger generation to have to put things right because the older generation has made a mess of things. The rising generation is not responsible for the existing state of the World.

On the other hand, the middle-aged generation is responsible for having brought the rising generation into the World and for having educated, or miseducated, or failed to educate, their children. So the rising generation is justified in being indignant if the parents' generation really has failed to fulfil the responsibility that, for the moment, is theirs because of their being temporarily in power. The generation that is in power is certainly blameworthy if, when 'the time is out of joint', this generation deliberately shuts its eyes to the truth and does not try to do anything to save the situation or tries only in a very perfunctory and incompetent way.

However, the older generation is blameworthy only to the extent that it truly has the power to make things better, but deliberately shirks its duty of using beneficently the amount of power that it does actually possess. There is a Sanskrit word which is a key word in Buddhism and which I should like to bring in here. This word is *karma*, and it means action in the special sense of the cumulative effect of all past actions. *Karma* limits human freedom; we are all in its grip. We do not start from scratch, we start with a past heritage; and the older generation's power is limited by the cumulative effect of all the actions of previous generations since the first appearance of life on this planet.

The limitedness of the power of the middle-aged generation is difficult for the rising generation to perceive. The rising generation sees that it is the victim of its parents' generation's failure, but it often does not see that its parents' generation is the victim of *karma*, and that the rising generation itself will become the victim of this same *karma* in its turn when it comes into power.

The present misunderstanding between generations is not surprising; it is perhaps inevitable, and the older generation ought to be charitable and forbearing towards the impatience and animosity of the young. The older generation has had the experience of having once been young and irresponsible; it is now responsible but at the same time is the victim of *karma* and is aware of this limitation of its freedom of action, however hard it may be trying, however eagerly it may be wishing, to make the World more like the World that the younger generation is demanding. I therefore think that it is for the older generation to take the initiative in trying to bring about a reconciliation between itself and the younger generation. But unhappily the present crisis in human history is so grave and so pressing that we cannot be sure that a reconciliation of the generations will be possible, even if the

on among the Confucians. Actually the Chinese
re building up something new.

movements, the hippy movement which is still un-
he militant student movement, are protests against
thority. Neither protest is new. Western university
perhaps as turbulent in the Middle Ages as they are
in the nineteenth century, German and Russian
ted against oppressive and benighted native authori-
al régimes, while Indian and Egyptian students
st colonial rule.

utmost goodwill, forbearance, and understanding is forthcoming
on both sides.

For at least five thousand years and perhaps longer, our increase
in power has been putting increasing pressure on us to control
ourselves individually and collectively. In our day, there is a split
in the rising generation over this issue. The present day radical/
militant students and the so-called 'hippies' are, as I see it, alternative manifestations of the distress of the present rising generation
at the disparity between the real and the ideal.

The militant students believe that society can be changed for
the better. They believe that their parents and grandparents have
failed to carry out the reforms that these older generations could
have made and ought to have made. They feel that there is no
time to be lost, because man has now acquired the power of
destroying human society—perhaps even destroying all life on
this planet—and therefore they feel that students must go into
immediate action to save society.

We would all agree that we need immediate action, but very
often it takes the form of violence. Why is this? The young—and
I sympathize with them in this—are caught in an agonizing
dilemma. If they demonstrate in an orderly, quiet, constitutional
way, they may get no attention whatever; older people may take
no notice, because they are busy and preoccupied with all kinds of
other concerns. If the young are violent, if they hit somebody,
hurt somebody, or, worst of all, kill somebody, then they will get
attention; but it may not be the kind of attention that they want,
or produce the results for which they were hoping. Violence committed by people who are protesting on behalf of reform often
provokes the so-called 'backlash' of reactionary forces. The student
who takes to violence meets the riot police, or the national guard,
armed with lethal weapons.

There is a lesson from history here to which I should like to
draw the attention of my younger contemporaries. History shows
that violent revolutions in the past have almost always provoked a
violent reaction. This either takes the form of a re-establishment
of the pre-revolutionary régime in a rather more unpleasant form
than before, or it takes the still more ironical form of the conversion

of the revolutionary régime itself into a caricature of the pre-revolutionary régime. There are many instances of the suppression of an insurrection or an attempted revolution by an 'establishment' which then takes Draconian measures to forestall another attempt. I need not elaborate this point. An example of the ironical consequences of a successful revolution is that of the Soviet régime, which is a caricature of the previous Tsarist régime. A famous nineteenth-century political philosopher, de Tocqueville, wrote a book demonstrating that the French Revolution did not abolish the Ancien Régime; it actually fulfilled it. The English, after their civil war in the seventeenth century, found Cromwell's rule even more oppressive than that of King Charles I, and I suspect that some Cubans may be finding life under Castro's rule more unpleasant than it was under the régime which he overthrew.

It is highly provocative when no attention is paid to demonstrations of a peaceful, constitutional kind; but do not let yourselves be provoked into using violence. If you take to violence, and if, in consequence, you are injured or killed, your fate will no doubt evoke sympathy from many people and will be generally deplored (though many people—perhaps most of an older generation than yours—will also feel that you brought it on yourselves). But in any case your fate is not likely to make the authorities in whom power is vested redress the evils which caused you to demonstrate in this way. They are certain to think, first and foremost, of their duty to maintain 'law and order'. They do, after all, owe it to the community as a whole to maintain 'law and order', though of course they lay themselves open to justifiable criticism if the agents whom they employ for this purpose use unnecessary force—and still more if the 'establishment' is convicted of exploiting its duty to restore order as a welcome opportunity for an indiscriminate repression of freedom and abrogation of human rights.

You may think that you are sacrificing yourselves in a just cause, but I want to make it clear that self-sacrifice as a result of taking the initiative in using violence is not what I mean by the self-sacrifice inspired by love to which I have referred earlier.

The 'hippies', unlike the militant students, seem to despair of being able to save society and are therefore trying to drop out of

society. This is apparently a ne
make what, in my view, is an
'hippies'. This is only the first
back to my hero, St. Francis of
day hippies in the United State
business man. His father had m
of his money, and he wanted
travagant way and to wear fir
that for a time, but he found i
he had a strong reaction. The
came to protest and St. Francis
his clothes in his father's face—a
of Assisi took this naked boy
The point that I am making is
a 'drop-out'—but he did not en
negative protest against his fa
went on to positive action; he
So I prefer not to judge the hi
the story.

There are many other exam
of great benefit to society. Tak
latter days of the Roman Empi
contemporaries they seemed
aroused the same sort of indign
American middle-aged, midd
ahead to later centuries you
really the founders of a new
which replaced the Graeco-Ro

In the sixth century, the Ben
world, but in a very positive
sleeping and eight hours prayii
largely agriculture. The restor
after its collapse at the end of tl

In China in the fourth an
Christian Era, when Buddh
there were drop-outs. People
cian civil servants became B

was ind
Buddhis
Both
finished
tradition
students
today, a
students
tarian p
agitated

3

Technology: A Generator of Wealth and of Problems

WAKAIZUMI: The volume of the natural resources consumed by industry has been increasing at a prodigious rate. The present figures are out of all proportion to any in the past. Are some of our indispensable natural resources in danger of being exhausted? Can the wasteful use of them be restrained? We have been ransacking and plundering the land surface of the globe. Can we make up for our prodigality on land by developing the resources of the sea? These submarine resources are still relatively intact.

Technology, reinforced by the application of science, has been producing wealth beyond our ancestors' dreams, but we have now begun to pay the price, and this is proving to be alarmingly high. Whether or not we are in danger of using up the planet's natural resources, it is certain that we are obliterating our natural environment by imposing on it a man-made one. We are polluting our habitat; we are also smothering it under a proliferation of apartment-houses, factories, and highways overloaded with noisy, fuming traffic. Might this be one of the causes of man's unhappiness and unrest, and his apparent aimlessness? Has the accelerating advance of technology perhaps outstripped man's social and spiritual life? How has this advance of technology aggravated the problem of power? Has it enabled us, or perhaps forced us, to face agonizing choices that were not within our ancestors' power and that may be beyond our present moral capacity? How do these banes of technology compare with its boons? How does the balance-sheet work out?

TOYNBEE: Are we in real danger of using up the natural resources of our planet? We have certainly been using them very fast since the Industrial Revolution. Having plundered the land surface of the Earth, shall we be able to get at the resources in the sea? This question is important, and it is rather alarming when we are confronted with comparative statistics of the present and the past rates of consumption of natural resources, especially those that are still indispensable for the maintenance and improvement of mankind's standard of material living. We must remember that, for three-quarters of the living generation, this standard is far too low, and yet we are using up our resources faster and faster.

It is true that in many cases the utilization of a once useful natural resource has been abandoned long before the supplies of this resource have been exhausted. The utilization of flint, for example, was abandoned, not because the supplies of flint ran short, but because the invention of metallurgy provided a substitute which was more efficient. There is plenty of flint left in the World, but it is now unlikely ever to be used. The same thing is happening now in the case of coal and is probably going to happen in the case of oil. My guess is that there will be a lot of coal and oil left over and never used, because man will have turned to using something else to cater for the same needs.

However, there are parts of the World—I am thinking particularly now of the Mediterranean basin, which I know fairly well—in which the once abundant supplies of timber have been exhausted; and in this case the consequences have been serious. There are substitutes for timber, and these are used successfully. Stone and brick and concrete can be and have been substituted for timber as materials for building on dry land. You cannot understand Ancient Greek architecture unless you realize that it is a translation into stone of forms of building which were designed originally for timber. But the Ancient Greeks did not find any substitute for timber for building ships. It was not until the nineteenth century that timber was replaced successfully by metal for shipbuilding. Moreover, the cutting down of forests to supply timber for buildings and ships has led in the Mediterranean basin to the erosion of the soil and to the desiccation of the climate. This is perhaps a special peril for certain regions. In climates with plenty of rainfall and grass—in Northern Europe, the Eastern United States, and also in Japan—deforestation need not cause erosion, and the replacement of forests by cereal-producing or rice-producing fields is a gain, so long as enough timber-producing forests are preserved. But to reafforest an eroded landscape is a slow, difficult. and expensive process of rehabilitating a natural environment that has been wrecked improvidently by human action. The advance of technology has placed the forest at man's mercy, reversing the original situation in which man was at the forest's mercy.

In the Ancient Italian religion, the god of forests, the god Silvanus, was also the god of international relations. This was because the areas inhabited and cultivated by human beings were originally simply clearings in a continuous forest. The forest made an insulator between one clearing and another. The god of forests became the god of international relations when the forests were gradually cleared and the inhabited clearings met; the rival makers of the clearings then began to fight each other for possession of the fields that had now replaced the forest. In his two capacities as the god of forests and god of international frontiers and relations, Silvanus embodies a whole chapter of Ancient Italian technological, economic, and political history.

Can man compensate for the irrevocable damage that he has done to nature on land? Can he make up for it by exploiting the sea? The greater part of the surface of our planet—a little more than two-thirds—is under water; and man's technology has been slower in achieving dominance here. To what extent can we cultivate the sea, as we began to cultivate the land eight or ten thousand years ago? So far, we have exploited the sea only in a Palaeolithic way. We have used the sea merely as a hunting ground for catching wild life. Can we replace fishing by breeding marine animals and marine plants? A start in the extension of agriculture and animal husbandry to the sea has been made in Japan, and the breeding of domesticated fish, as a substitute for hunting wild fish, has been practised on rivers and in lakes and in artificial ponds for a long time in many parts of the World. Can the techniques already in use for farming inland waters be applied to the sea on any scale that would substantially increase the World's food supply?

I do not have the scientific and technological knowledge needed for answering this important question. I am simply guessing when I suggest that the farming of the sea seems likely to be practicable in the shallow seas that cover the Continental Shelf. But this fringe of the sea is only a small area in comparison with the extent of the deep sea, and I do not know what the prevailing opinion is, among the experts, about the possibility of exploiting the riches of the deep sea. However, I do notice that the experts are alarmed at the extent to which the sea is already being polluted by the discharge into rivers of man-made poisonous substances (pesticides, refuse from factories, and so on). If we do not become more responsible-minded, we may find that we have ruined even the deep sea as a potential source of food.

While the sea itself is a potential source of food supply, the planet's solid surface below the sea bottom is a potential field for extracting minerals. The greatest of our still untapped reserves of minerals, both solid and liquid, must lie below the bottom of the sea. To what extent are these submarine mineral deposits going to prove accessible for human mining-engineers?

There is one consideration about the potential future exploitation of the sea that is of prime political importance. Up till now, only a fringe of the sea has been claimed by the adjacent local states as being part of the domain that they consider to be under their sovereignty. The British Government used to insist on there being a three-mile limit to so-called 'territorial waters'; to insist that everything beyond three miles distance from any country's coast was no-man's water and therefore belonged to everybody. Even if the standard breadth of these 'territorial waters' were to be extended to 200 miles—and this has been done by the Peruvians, I believe—by far the greater part of the sea, and even a considerable part of the shallow seas covering the Continental Shelf, would still remain unclaimed by any local state and would therefore be claimable by mankind collectively as a public domain for a future world state.

I should like to see this claim accepted by the World's present sovereign local states. This would provide a future world government with an independent revenue of its own, and it would also provide a fund for raising the material standard of living of the poor majority of the World's population. These two services could then be financed without asking for contributions from the local states. This would be a big step towards knitting the human race together into a single family. But here again the preservation of mankind's common patrimony is being imperilled by the greed of competing nations.

In our time man has been violating and desecrating non-human nature all over the World. This has been the cumulative effect of two distinct though interrelated causes. One cause has been the accelerating advance of technology; the other has been the population explosion, which the advance of technology has made possible. Man's conquest of nature has been brilliant, but his misuse of his victory has been tragic. Our violation of nature has been haphazard and blind; we have been destroying nature's beauty, and, by polluting her, have turned her into a menace once again. I can see what is happening in my own country, which was once so beautiful. I have seen it happening in Japan. You can see it in America, where the virgin wilderness has been changed into slums. You can see it all over the World. I have touched already on what man's proper relation to nature should be, and I shall be returning again to this vital matter in my answers to the questions about religion.

Man awoke to consciousness in an environment in which he found himself parked, or tethered, or planted—whichever word you like to use—but which he had not made for himself. At the start, man was at the mercy of his natural environment. He had to struggle to feed himself with whatever food he could gather or catch; he had to try to escape being exterminated by other wild beasts; and he had to hold his own against the weather, against heat and cold, against drought and flood. To begin with, man's habitat, we are told, was confined to warm regions, because his ancestors had shed their fur, and also it was more difficult for early man to cross rivers and mountains and forests and morasses, not to speak of trying to cross the sea, than it is for his present-day descendants to fly over the North Pole or to reach the Moon. So early men could not spread round the globe easily or quickly.

However, since man became human, he has been consciously and deliberately changing his original natural environment into an artificial man-made environment. This is what we mean by the progress of technology. The oldest relics of human life are not human bones. Very ancient human bones are rare. The earliest relics of human life are tools, which, even from the earliest ages, are relatively abundant. When I say tools, I do not mean natural objects used as tools in an unmodified state. Non-human animals —for instance, some of the apes and beavers and sea-otters—use unmodified natural objects as tools. I have seen sea-otters prizing limpets or other shellfish off rocks by picking up stones and breaking the shellfish off, but they do not chip those stones to make a sharper edge. They take the stones as they find them. The great advance that our ancestors made, right at the beginning of the present human phase of our history, was that they modified natural objects in order to turn them into more efficient tools for modifying other natural objects. For instance, a man found that a chipped stone was a better tool than an unchipped stone for felling a tree or for killing a wild goat.

During the first million years of human history, technology was virtually static. We can see this for ourselves by visiting any museum of prehistoric remains. We find that the same tools of practically the same pattern continued to be used all over the World for about a million years. When a tool was invented, it spread extremely slowly, because people could only carry the tool on foot and hand it to other people a few miles off, and it might take years before these decided to imitate it. But at this stage technology changed so slowly that there was time for a uniform pattern of tools to spread all over the World, just as a uniform pattern of tools spreads like lightning today owing to our so-called 'annihilation of distance' through the improvement of means of communication. The pattern now changes quickly, but the spread round the globe of each successive modification is still more rapid.

Our 5,000 years of civilization is a very short period compared with the previous first million years of pre-civilizational human history, but, within these last 5,000 years—and last 10,000 and last 30,000 years—the pace of man's progressive increase in ability to change the universe has been accelerating. Why do I mention 5,000, 10,000, 30,000 years? The dawn of civilization was about 5,000 years ago. Ten thousand years ago: that was the date of the beginning of the Neolithic Age. The name is rather misleading. We call it the Neolithic Age because of the new way of making tools that our ancestors discovered at that stage. Instead of chipping stones to make sharp edges, they found out how to grind stones to the exact shape that they wanted. That was a very important technological invention; but much more important, as marking the beginning of the Neolithic Age, was the invention of agriculture, the domestication of animals, the invention of spinning and weaving, the invention of pottery, the invention of boats. Before the end of the Neolithic Age, in the fifth and fourth millennia B.C., when the earliest of the civilizations had not yet arisen, our ancestors invented the mining, extracting, and working of metals. The beginnings of writing also date from this period, and so, perhaps, does the use of wind in sails for driving ships.

Thirty thousand years ago: that was the date of the transition from the Lower Palaeolithic Age, by far the longest period of man's history so far, to the relatively short Upper Palaeolithic Age. This Upper Palaeolithic Age lasted for about 20,000 years, and during that time man made what was a relatively sudden advance in the form of his tools by improved methods of flaking.

What we call the Industrial Revolution (the scientific foundations for which were laid in the seventeenth century) has not really been the first industrial revolution in human history. The distinctive characteristic of the Industrial Revolution which started in Britain 200 years ago and which is still going on at an accelerating pace today is that human and animal muscle-power has finally been replaced by inanimate energy as a physical motive force. Wind-power was harnessed perhaps 5,000 years ago for driving ships, and water-power was harnessed perhaps about 2,000 years ago for working water-mills, but the systematic and exclusive use of inanimate power is what we mean when we speak of the Industrial Revolution in the modern world.

Technological progress has been cumulative, and it is likely to continue to be cumulative, in the sense that a technological achievement, once made, is not lost again, and that the next achievement is based on what has been achieved already. Technology has been advancing at an accelerating pace ever since the beginning of the Upper Palaeolithic Age about 30,000 years ago, but it has been advancing in jerks, not at an even pace, and within the last 200 years it has started on a new spurt forward. Though this is not an unprecedented phenomenon, the current spurt is unprecedented in its potency. It has finally reversed the original relation between man and non-human nature. Since the Industrial Revolution, man has made himself the master of non-human nature, and this apparently once for all, irreversibly, unless man were to re-liberate non-human nature by destroying himself. Man's successors and heirs might then be the social insects, who are more ancient than man is and might be longer-lived for all we know.

Man's achievement of gaining the mastery over non-human nature has been bought at the price of enslaving himself to a new artificial man-made environment. This new environment is more uncongenial, tyrannical, and psychologically disturbing than the old one, and this exchange is one of the causes of the present world-wide unrest, conflict, violence, and mutual frustration of human wills. There have been frequent bouts in the past of a similar loss of concord and consequent loss of control over human affairs, though perhaps none of these previous bouts went to such extremes as the present one.

Of all the countries that I have visited, Japan affords the most striking example of the replacement of man's natural environment by a man-made environment. My first visit to Japan was in 1929. My ship stopped for the inside of a day at the Shimonoseki Straits, leading to the Inland Sea, and I also visited Nara among other places. When I visit the Shimonoseki Straits and Nara now, I can hardly recognize either of them, because the natural landscape which existed in 1929—fields, hedges, trees—has been obliterated by apartment-houses, offices, factories, and streets. What is happening in Japan gives you a preview of what is going to happen, on the Japanese scale, all over the World.

Man has revolutionized his natural environment in order to try to make this natural environment conform to his requirements. Man has mastered nature, but, in doing that, he has enslaved himself to the new man-made environment that he has conjured up all round him. Man has condemned himself now to live in cities and to make his living by working in factories and offices.

This urban work is physically easier than cultivating the soil or looking after flocks and herds of domesticated animals, and it is a great deal easier physically than hunting or fishing or gathering edible fruits and roots and grubs. All that was very hard labour. But urban work is much more monotonous. Hunting was more dangerous, and the food supply won by hunting was more precarious than the product of mechanized farming. But spraying insecticide is not so exciting as shooting or trapping a mammoth or a mastodon or as harpooning a whale, and it is noticeable that people who have the time to spare and have the necessary money go hunting and fishing for sport. They have a nostalgia for their prehistoric past—for the million years during which hunting and fishing were the occupations by which our ancestors made their living.

We have seen that mankind's present experience of revolutionary change is not unprecedented and that mankind has managed to survive previous revolutionary changes which came upon him with equal speed and with equal intensity. There is some comfort in reminding ourselves of this. It may give us courage and hope in our present crisis.

The most astonishing of the revolutionary changes in our time is the increase in material wealth through the application of science to technology. In this, our scientifically-planned technology has been successful beyond all expectations. But this success, so far from ensuring human happiness, has actually not increased it. Since the very beginning of civilization, wealth has been unequally distributed, and the inequality has not been overcome by the productivity of the modern Industrial Revolution. Today the richest of the industrialized countries is the United States, but, even there, one-tenth, or perhaps one-fifth, of the population is still wretchedly poor and ill-cared for, and the countries in which a part of the population has become rich are only a minority. Three-quarters of the world's population still consists of peasants whose standard of material life is not much higher than the standard of the Neolithic Age.

Moreover, the minority of the human race which has now become rich has bought its wealth at a high price in terms of loss of freedom and loss of happiness. The Palaeolithic hunter was freer than his successor, the Neolithic peasant, but the peasant at least still found pleasure in his work. He loved his crops and he loved his domesticated animals. The handicraft manufacturer, in the literal sense of a maker of things by hand, not by machinery, also took pleasure in his work, and took pride, too, in doing his work well. But the present-day urban industrial worker and office worker is less free than his predecessors, the handicraft worker and the peasant, and his work is monotonous. He tends to live, there-fore, not for his work, but for the money that he makes by his work, and for recreation. 'Recreation' is a very significant word. *Re*-creation: the suggestion is that work dis-creates the worker, that it makes him sub-human or non-human, and that therefore he has to spend his time when off work in making himself human again. Before the Industrial Revolution, work itself was recreation, so the worker did not need recreation in his spare time.

This divorce between work and zest makes for unhappiness. Look at the Palaeolithic hunters' paintings, now perhaps 25,000–30,000 years old, in the caves in France and Spain. Here they have painted the animals that they hunted, and the paintings show that Palaeolithic man had immense zest for the occupation by which he made his living. The animals are drawn marvellously true to life, and you can see the eagerness with which the hunter, and the painter looking over the hunter's shoulder, was getting the im-pression of the animals and studying every detail of each animal's shape and colour and movements. He was fascinated by the animals that he was hunting. The Palaeolithic hunter lacked all our present-day material amenities, but he was probably happier than we are. We cannot talk to him, but we can gaze at his paintings, and these throw light on his feelings.

Until now, man has become the prisoner of each of the techno-logical advances that he has achieved. He has become their prisoner because each advance has been followed by an increase in population. There was probably a population-explosion at the end of the Lower Palaeolithic Age; there certainly was one at the beginning of the Neolithic Age; and there has been a tremendous one since the beginning of the Industrial Revolution. With this increased population, mankind would starve if we attempted to retreat to our previous way of life, which, in each case, was technologically less efficient but may perhaps have been spiritually more satisfying. The Industrial Revolution has caught us again in the same old way. Owing to the present population-explosion, we shall not be able to escape from the urban life or from the factory-work and the office-work to which we have condemned ourselves by making the Industrial Revolution. We have to accept the urban destiny that we have decreed for ourselves. What we must try to do is to make this destiny as tolerable as we can manage.

What vision do I have of the future? Anyone who lives or works in Tokyo, or who lives outside Tokyo and goes in and out of Tokyo every day, or who has ever visited Tokyo as a foreigner, will be alarmed at the prospect of life in the city. I have been in Tokyo as recently as 1967, and it seems to me that, in present-day Tokyo, we have a preview of what the city of the future may become if we fail to take steps in time to give the development of the World's cities a radical new orientation. The people who are concerned with the administration of Tokyo are trying with all their might to do this at the present time. The same effort is being made by the administrators of all the World's other great cities.

We cannot undo city life, we cannot prevent it, but perhaps we can humanize it. I have thought much about my vision of the future city. I foresee a nightmare future unless we can forestall this by taking remedial action in good time. We need to plan now for dates that are still many years ahead.

How are we to humanize the city? I should like to see the city of the future broken up into a large number of small self-contained sub-units. Call them 'wards' or 'parishes' or whatever you like. These wards ought to be small enough for the inmates of them to be personally acquainted with each other, to be, in fact, neighbours in the social sense, not merely in the topographical sense. In a large city we often live next door to people whom we never meet. In the block of flats in London in which Professor Wakaizumi and I exchanged ideas, many people frequently go up and down in the elevator, but we seldom meet each other; we do not all know each other personally. This is unnatural; yet it is typical of present-day city life. We need to change this into a real neighbourliness in the sense of being each other's friends and doing things for each other.

The sub-divisions of the city ought to be self-contained to a degree that will make it possible for the children to go to school and for the wives and mothers to do their shopping and their washing without having to cross any road that is infested with dangerous mechanized vehicles.

This is not a Utopian idea. It is a practicable and indispensable lay-out for the coming world city. We need a new name for a new thing. It has been labelled Ecumenopolis, a Greek word which means the city that embraces the whole Ecumenê, the whole habitable world. The wards of this Ecumenopolis ought each to be a replica of an Ancient Greek city-state, and the world city would consist of hundreds and thousands of sub-divisions, each of the size of an Ancient Greek city-state or of a medieval Italian or German or Flemish city-state, or of eighteenth-century Frankfurt, in which the German poet Goethe was brought up, or of the medieval city of Sakai, which was a Japanese city-state. That is the standard size of the city of the pre-Industrial Revolution age. There have, of course, been bigger cities, but they have been rare exceptions till the Industrial Revolution gave birth to cities of a gigantic size. The sub-divisions of Ecumenopolis ought not to be bunched together; they ought to be strung out, so that each of them will have access to a zone of country that will be un-built-up and will be kept open permanently.

Since the Second World War, some of these ideals have been translated into practical reality in two places that I have seen. Some years ago I was at Karachi, the old capital of Pakistan, and I was taken out to see the housing estates outside Karachi, in which the Muslim refugees from India were being housed. (No doubt round New Delhi I could have seen the Hindu refugees from Pakistan being rehoused: I just happened to see the re-housing near Karachi.) These housing estates were laid out in small groups. They were planted on a large level plain, and they stretched away and away, one group after another. Each group had a school and a mosque and a place for washing clothes and a little market-place where people could all get together and talk. This lay-out had been deliberately designed by a Greek town-planner, Dr. Constantine Doxiadis, who had been invited by the Government of Pakistan to plan the re-housing of the refugees. He found a way in which it was possible for them to strike root again, and, when I met Dr. Doxiadis afterwards and asked him how he had known how to make this possible, he said: 'Because my family were refugees, and I have had the experience.' He knew about this at first hand, so he knew what needed doing.

I have also visited Brasilia, the new capital of Brazil. Brasilia was planned no longer ago than about 1960 and the building started a year or two later. Brasilia was built right out in the wilderness, deliberately. To begin with, they had to fly in even the concrete by air, because there was no road or railway leading to the site. In Brasilia you have a working example of some of the reforms which make a great modern city more tolerable. If you go up on to the roof of a high building in Brasilia and look down, you will see a completely even flow of traffic; no traffic jams. Why? Because there are no level crossings and no traffic-lights. All the roads have an underpass or an overpass, and you are never held up while a stream of traffic at right angles to yours is having to make its way across your route.

Moveover, in Brasilia, a large part of the city is divided into what they call 'quadras', that is squares. Each 'quadra' contains a number of apartment-houses. It also contains an open space and schools and shops and automat laundries, so that the wives and mothers and children can spend the whole of their day inside the 'quadra' without ever having to cross a road with motorized traffic on it. Children can go to school and come back from school by themselves. No one has to guide them across dangerous roads. The women do not have to go far to do their shopping. They do not have to stand in queues. Of course, they can, if they choose, go longer distances to bigger and grander shops; and I suppose that, when the children go to the university, they will have to go out of their 'quadra' and along streets with traffic in them; and the men, and the women who have professional work, will have to leave the 'quadra' during working hours. But, thanks to the 'quadra' plan, a large part of the population is able, for most of the time, to escape from having to contend with motorized traffic. There is also a more important and positive advantage. The people living in the same 'quadra' can become each other's neighbours and friends. They can know each other and know about each other's lives. Life in a 'quadra' in Brasilia is like life in an ancient city-state or in a village; and yet the 'quadra' is in the middle of a city of three-quarters of a million people already—a city that is going to grow much bigger.

Here is one suggestion for curing the loneliness of the so-called 'lonely crowd', a suggestion for enabling the multitudes who are streaming out of the rural countryside into the city to strike root in their unfamiliar new urban environment. Am I too optimistic in believing that a decentralization of the world city, on the lines that I have been illustrating by the examples of the new settlements outside Karachi and the 'quadras' in Brasilia, might make life in the world city endurable, and this even for those city-dwellers—and these will be the majority—whose parents were peasants of an almost Neolithic type?

Rural immigrants into the city can acclimatize themselves to city life. I can illustrate this from my own family history. My grandfather on my father's side was a farmer's son, born in 1810. He left the countryside in which his ancestors had lived for at least a thousand years. He had been brought up on a farm in a part of England which the Danes had conquered 1,100 years ago, and I suppose the family had been living there on the land as agricultural labourers or as farmers ever since then. Suddenly, my grandfather's generation came to the city and my grandfather became a doctor in London. My father became a social worker. So three generations of my family have now been urban workers, including myself. And yet our family has managed to survive this enormous revolution of moving from an agricultural environment into the entirely alien environment of London, which in my grandfather's generation was already beginning to grow by leaps and bounds to its present gigantic size. Yet, as I say, we have survived.

4

Religion: A Perennial Need?

WAKAIZUMI: What is the future of religion? Does religion have a future? It is often said that in the past, religion has, at least to some extent, enabled man to deal with human problems in a human way. The spiritual life of faith, it is contended, is superior to the material life of abundance. Yet today religion seems to be losing its hold, especially over the rising generation. The young are either indifferent to religion or are positively disillusioned with it and mistrustful of it. Meanwhile, science has been making statements that are verifiable by experiment. Is science taking over from religion the role of giving man knowledge and guidance for taking his bearings in the universe? Historically most religions have claimed that they can give man answers to the riddle of death, or at least console him; and help him overcome his fears. Can equivalent help be found in science, and in the astonishingly successful application of science to technology?

One of the fundamental tenets of religion seems to be that there is a spiritual force greater than man. Is this postulate compatible with verified scientific truth? Whether it is compatible with science or not, can man live without making this postulate?

Different accounts of the spiritual life are given by different religions. Does this variety of doctrine cast doubt on all religious doctrines alike, or would this be a mistaken conclusion? The religions have differed much less from each other in their commandments than in their doctrine. Would you say that there is a relative consensus about what is right and wrong?

What is the distinction between religion and philosophy? Is it right to see a hierarchy of religions or beliefs? Is there a place for the ancient worship of nature in a world in which man is obliterating his natural environment by imposing a man-made one on it? How does the rise of nationalism affect mankind's prospects? Do you see nationalism as a kind of religion, or perhaps as something which has replaced religion in the modern world?

The new environment that man has conjured up for himself through his science and his technology may call for radical changes in his social institutions. Can institutions be changed radically on a scientific basis? Is there room for the old religious values in some new guise?

TOYNBEE: When a human being wakes to consciousness as a child, he finds that he has been planted in a universe which is a mystery to him, and that he has been placed in this universe without ever being consulted, or ever having been asked for his permission. In the immediate sense, he was planted in the universe by his parents, but who planted his parents and their predecessors there? This is a mystery which goes back to the nature of the reality behind the universe. Why are we here? What are we here for? The only thing about the universe that is clear to a human being is that it has him at its mercy. He soon learns that, besides having been born perforce, he is going to have to die perforce sooner or later. Of course, non-human living creatures face the same situation, but they are not aware of it as we are. Our human awareness of it is disturbing; and this disturbance stimulates our curiosity. We want to know what the universe is; how and why the universe has come into existence; why a human being does find himself in the universe for the very brief period of a human lifetime. We want to know whether we were in existence before we were born into this world and whether we are going to go on existing after our death. We want to make up our minds whether life is a blessing or a curse. All these questions force themselves upon us as soon as we become conscious, and religion, as I see it, is an attempt to find answers to these insistent questions. Religion is an attempt to discover how to reconcile ourselves to the formidable facts of life and death.

I have mentioned that technological progress, though it has been cumulative, has proceeded discontinuously, in a series of spurts or waves. There have also been waves of spiritual progress. I think this simile of 'waves' is illuminating. It is significant that the two chief waves of spiritual progress occurred in the period of about 5,000 years, ending in the outbreak of the Industrial Revolution in the eighteenth century, during which technology was relatively stagnant. What have been these 'waves' of spiritual progress?

The first of them was at the dawn of civilization, and it was this that made civilization possible. This wave of spiritual progress was not caused or accompanied or followed by any noteworthy advance in technology. The first wave of spiritual progress was the fruit of an advance in sociality. I think that civilization was made possible by the co-operation of human beings in large numbers for performing large-scale public works: drainage, irrigation, the building of temples and of tombs. This work was done, not for the immediate personal profit of the individuals who carried it out, but for distant returns for society in general. We do not know the religious background of the rise of civilization; we can only guess about it. As soon as civilization comes into existence, we begin to get temples and, with the invention of writing, we get records in the form of religious liturgies and religious lyrics or epics; and my guess is that the rise of civilization does imply the presence of religious faith directed by leaders who had a vision of the future and who had a genius for organization, and for persuading their fellow human beings to submit to being organized for working on long-term projects which would bring in only distant returns. That was, in my opinion, the first wave of spiritual progress, and the fruit of it was what we call civilization.

The second wave of spiritual progress was the rise of what I call the 'higher' religions and philosophies, and this wave ran from about the eighth century B.C.—that is the date of the earliest Israelite prophets—down to the seventh century of the Christian Era, which is the date of the Prophet Muhammad. A number of people have put their finger on this second wave. They have called it the 'Axis Age', in the sense of a hinge on which the whole of human history turns. The emergence of the 'higher' religions makes a dividing line, as, in the Christian presentation of history, the distinction between B.C. and A.D. makes a clean cut between a 'before' and an 'after' in human history. Certainly human history has never been the same again since these 'higher' religions came into existence.

Some people have given a more closely limited extension to the Axis Age. They have held that the Axis Age was limited to the sixth century B.C. In this century there was a remarkable galaxy of contemporary spiritual geniuses and founders of religions and philosophies. It was the century of the Buddha, of Laotse, of Confucius, of the Iranian prophet Zarathustra, and of the anonymous 'Second Isaiah', who is, to modern minds, the greatest of all the Israelite prophets, and whose work is tacked on to the book of the genuinely historical Isaiah who wrote in the eighth century B.C. But, in my belief, the Axis Age, the second wave of mankind's spiritual advance, is longer than a single century. It seems to me to extend from the eighth century B.C. to the mission of Muhammad in the seventh century of the Christian Era.

My hope is that we shall see a period of technological slowing-down and a new wave of spiritual advance. As a result of the present rapid development of the natural sciences and technology, they have become dominant in the life of the present generation of the human race, and this raises the question of the relation between the material side of human life and the spiritual side. I believe, with complete conviction, without hesitation or qualification, that man is a spiritual being; but he is also a physical organism who finds himself in a universe that has a material as well as a spiritual facet. He must therefore seek to provide himself with as much material apparatus as he needs for leading the highest possible spiritual life.

I have used the word 'highest'. It is interesting that all our vocabulary about spiritual things is metaphorical. It is transferred from physical things. We say 'high' because we have no word except this word for physical elevation to convey spiritual sublimity (and sublime, too, originally means just 'high'). This shows how dominant the physical aspect of life is for us, and therefore how important it is for us to keep the physical and the spiritual in proper balance. This is especially important because nature has endowed man with much greater ability for understanding and mastering non-human nature than for mastering himself, learning how to live in peace and friendship with his fellows, and putting himself in spiritual harmony with the presence behind the universe. There is a great inequality in the degree of man's giftedness for science and technology on the one hand and for religion and sociality on the other hand, and this is, to my mind, one of man's chief discords, misfortunes, and dangers. Human nature is out of balance.

There has always been a 'morality gap', like the 'credibility gap' of which some politicians have been accused. We could justly accuse the whole human race, since we became human, of a 'morality gap', and this gap has been growing wider as technology has been making cumulative progress while morality has been stagnating. Technology gives us material power, and this is morally neutral; it can be used, at will, for either good or evil. The greater our material power, the greater our need for the spiritual insight and virtue to use our power for good and not for evil. Material power that is not counterbalanced by adequate spiritual power, that is, by love and wisdom, is a curse and not a blessing. The less we have of it the better. The 'morality gap' means that, since we first became human, we have never been adequate spiritually for handling our material power; and today the morality gap is, I suppose, greater than it has ever been in any previous age.

Governments are aggravating this disparity today by subsidizing science and technology for the further development of material power, because material power produces wealth and military might, and these are the assets that make for success in the power-competition among this planet's 140 or so sovereign independent states. But to seek this kind of success is short-sighted; it is bound to end in disaster for all the participants, including the victors, in the future world war to which this power-competition is likely to lead if it remains unchecked. Actually, the word 'victor' has become meaningless, because a future world war would be an atomic war, and in nuclear warfare there would be no victors, only victims. The morality gap has caused a number of civilizations to come to grief. Surely we ought to make our governments reverse their present policy of subsidizing science and research as instruments for the political and military power-competition. Scientific and technological achievements cannot be undone, but at least from now on we could, if we chose, divert our efforts and our energies from science and technology to religion and ethics.

We human beings are tragically incompetent and unsuccessful in dealing with ourselves. Yet, of all the things with which we have to deal, our own human nature is the most perverse and the most intractable, while at the same time it is also the most important. Therefore we ought to give first priority to trying to learn how to deal more successfully with ourselves. Human greed will take care that we use our practical abilities for giving ourselves the wherewithal to deal with the material side of life.

The existence of the morality gap and the importance of closing it has been recognized by the world's spiritual geniuses. The teachings of the Buddha do not differ in this respect from those of the Chinese philosophers Confucius and Laotse, or of the Ancient Greek philosophers Socrates and Zeno (the founder of the Stoic philosophy), or of all the Hebrew prophets from Amos in the eighth century B.C. to Jesus. These spiritual leaders were manifestly on the right track. We ought to follow their lead today.

In one of a number of imaginary dialogues, Socrates' pupil, Plato, who was also a great philosopher in his own right, presents the history of Socrates' life in the form of an autobiographical reminiscence which may or may not be true. Plato makes Socrates say: when I was young I was interested in the current fashionable philosophy, which was physical science, physics and astronomy, and geology. (I am using modern words, but these are the sciences that Plato means. The embryo of physics and geology, and more than the embryo of astronomy, existed in the fifth century B.C.) But Socrates goes on to say: I came to realize that the important thing in the universe is human beings, not non-human nature, not the movements of the stars and not the nature of the chemical elements and so on. What is important is the human spirit, so I decided that I would turn away from the study of non-human nature and would study why it is that men know what is good but do what is bad. And I would study this not just out of curiosity but in order to help myself and to help my fellow human beings to become better people than we are. I believe that this change in Socrates' intellectual orientation, as Plato reports it, is an historical fact, and I feel that it is very significant. It was certainly a turning point, not only in Ancient Greek thought, but also in Ancient Greek morality and life.

I should like to see some modern Socrates redirect the spirit of the modern world, perhaps not entirely away from science and technology, but make it give first priority to studying our human selves. The reason why the World is in its present dangerous condition is not because of any failure of science and technology. We have created, by our application of science to technology, some enormously effective and powerful tools. We have not the spiritual power or understanding or goodness to use these tools right, so we are rightly afraid that we may use them to destroy ourselves. We need another Socrates.

The World in our time is being dehumanized, and this is distressing. We need to humanize, or let me say to re-humanize, our education, and I think this requires a new ideology, and not only a new educational ideology. To be effective, it must be a new philosophical and religious outlook, covering the whole of life. It must be a change in our ideals, bringing with it a change in the order of our priorities. This is the important point.

At present we are very successfully giving priority to the achievement of wealth and power, but our success is not giving us satisfaction and it is bringing us into danger. We are purchasing these commodities (I call them 'commodities' on purpose, because they are material things) at the price of individual unhappiness for ourselves and of discord with each other. The early eighteenth-century English poet Pope wrote the famous line 'The proper study of mankind is man.' Pope is surely right. We ought to study man for the purpose of making ourselves better and making our relations with each other better.

In any field of human endeavour, stagnation and regression and advance are all equally possible at any stage. The reason why science has advanced so portentously within the last three centuries, and technology within the last two centuries, is because a larger number of people than ever before have taken up these activities. Ability has flowed into these channels, and the liberal arts and professions have languished, because they have been relatively unfashionable. I believe that it has been estimated that about ninety-seven per cent of all the scientists who have ever lived are alive at this moment. But suppose that, in the next generation, the ablest minds and the most perceptive spirits were to come to Socrates' conclusion. Suppose that they were to conclude that the most urgent business on mankind's agenda was, not to push the advance of science and technology forward still farther, but to close the morality gap, or at any rate to make it a little less wide than it is today.

I think this is not only possible but probable. Already, in the universities of the United States, I believe that some students on the eve of graduation are declining offers of secure and well-paid jobs in the service of business corporations, and are looking, instead, for careers that will be of greater social and spiritual value for mankind, and will therefore also be more satisfying, psychologically, than careers followed, not for their own sake, but for the sake of the money that they bring in. If this new scale of values prevails, religion and the arts will flourish, and science and technology will languish. In the rich countries we have more than enough, now, of material power and wealth.

Man's spiritual side, which has infinite potentialities, will be given scope for the first time in his history when his material needs, which are limited, have been fully catered for, in the poorer, undeveloped countries as well as in the rich ones, by technology's extraordinarily rapid modern advance. We have chosen to label our species, not *homo faber*, man the technician, but *homo sapiens*, man the wise. We have not earned this self-conferred title *homo sapiens*. We have shown little wisdom, so far, in controlling ourselves and in managing our relations with each other. If we succeed in surviving the present technological revolution, we may at last become *homo sapiens* in truth as well as in name.

We have discussed the dehumanizing effects of technology, but we have not yet discussed the questions whether religion can provide an antidote to these dehumanizing effects, whether man can live without religion, and whether the established forms of religion will continue to satisfy man's spiritual needs. In my belief, science and technology cannot serve as substitutes for religion. They cannot satisfy the spiritual needs for which religion of all kinds does try to provide, though they may discredit some of the traditional dogmas of the so-called 'higher' religions.

Historically, religion came first and science grew out of religion. Science has never superseded religion, and it is my expectation

that it never will supersede it. Science demands definite, incontro-
vertible answers to the questions that science asks, but the questions
that are of the greatest concern to human beings cannot be
answered with any certainty. I think the reason why science does
succeed in answering its questions is that the questions which it
asks are not the most important ones. In pointing out the limits of
what science can do, I am not depreciating science's achievements
within its own field. Many distinguished scientists have antici-
pated me in expressing this opinion, and their judgement is
authoritative.

Before the rise of science, religion gave unscientific answers to
some of the relatively unimportant questions with which science
has now concerned itself. Many of religion's answers to these
questions have been refuted by science's answers to them. Science
has answered these questions by investigation and by experiment
in a convincing way which is different from the unproven traditional religious answers to the same scientific questions. In so far
as the ecclesiastical authorities—the religious 'establishments', I
will call them—have tried to maintain traditional religious answers
after science has refuted these answers, the ecclesiastics have
brought religion into disrepute, and the consequent distrust of,
and disillusionment with, established religion has been to that
extent deserved. But science has not taken up religion's fundamental questions, or, if it has taken these up, it has not given
genuine scientific answers to them. It has reproduced the traditional religious answers in non-religious language, and these
pseudo-scientific answers are not really more illuminating than
the traditional answers.

For instance, early Greek science is really Greek mythology
translated into terms of physical and psychic forces, and it is easy
to translate these forces back into gods and goddesses. Marxian
sociology is Jewish and Christian mythology in very thin disguise.
The Darwinian theory of evolution is an attempt to account for
creation without using the anthropomorphic concept of a God
who makes things in the way in which human beings make things.
We cannot believe any longer that the universe was made in the
way in which a blacksmith or a carpenter makes things, but we

have not yet found a genuine alternative explanation. I do not think that the Darwinian theory of evolution has given a positive account of an alternative way in which the universe may have been brought into existence.

Science has been most successful so far in dissecting the structure and explaining the working of inanimate nature. It has been less successful in doing the same for organic nature. It has had some success in analysing the workings of conscious human thought. As early as the fifth century B.C. the Indians and the Greeks were studying logic and epistemology, that is to say, the workings of the conscious rational human mind; and recently, in my own lifetime, modern man has begun to probe into the workings of the unconscious part of the psyche, the vast gulf that lies below the thin layer of consciousness.

The deliberate systematic application of science to technology has made it possible for technology to advance farther in the last 300 years than during the previous million years during which technology was empirical—that is to say, was working from hand to mouth by trial and error. Applied to living material organisms, science has done wonders in the fields of surgery and medicine and in breeding new varieties of non-human animals and of plants. Science has also begun to find out how to cure psychic sickness. So far, however, science has shown no signs that it is going to be able to cope with man's most serious problems. It has not been able to do anything to cure man of his sinfulness and his sense of insecurity, or to avert the painfulness of failure and the dread of death. Above all, it has not helped him to break out of the prison of his inborn self-centredness into communion or union with some reality that is greater, more important, more valuable, and more lasting than the individual himself.

Moreover, the solution of some human problems by the application of science to technology creates other problems. Suppose that science were to succeed one day in making human beings immortal; the dread of death would then be removed, but it might be replaced by a longing for death. Death sets a time-limit to the liability created by a human life for the person himself and for his contemporaries, especially his younger contemporaries. So far, science has only succeeded in lengthening the expectation of life, and this has proved a doubtful blessing; for, although science has relieved physical pain, it has not yet discovered how to make the aged immune from senility, or how to shield them from loneliness and from anxiety if they still retain their wits.

So, though the successes of science and technology have been sensational, I am still more impressed by the limitations of what they can do for mankind. Our greatest need is for a spiritual improvement in ourselves and in our relations with our fellow human beings, but this is a need that science and technology in themselves cannot meet. It is well known that physical nature cannot bear a physical vacuum, and the same is true of the spiritual facet of the universe as well. Science and technology may create a religious vacuum by bringing previously accepted religions into discredit, but they cannot fill this vacuum themselves; it will be filled by religions of some kind.

I do not believe that any human being has ever been without religion or ever can be. To feel reverence and awe seems to be one of the inborn instincts of human beings; they feel the need to look beyond themselves to some supernatural or natural being or power, or even to do obeisance to some particular object such as the flag which has become the symbol of nationhood. I think this feeling persists among many people who pride themselves on their rationalism, though they may be unconscious of it. But a human being who is normally unconscious of his religion is apt to feel the need for it at moments of personal crisis. Personal crises are inevitable, especially the final crisis of death. Even people who die instantaneously—in an accident, for instance—and have therefore not been aware of the approach of death, are unlikely to have got through life without meeting with personal crises of some kind. Even if theirs has been a short life, so that they have not had to cope with the special problems created by old age, it is almost certain that they will have had to face up to some difficulties for which science and technology have not provided a solution.

I am convinced, myself, that man's fundamental problem is his human egocentricity. He dreams of making the universe a desirable place for himself, with plenty of free time, relaxation, security, and good health, and with no hunger or poverty. Every individual living creature of every species is egocentric. That is true even of species which are social, like human beings or wolves or beavers, in which the individual cannot live in isolation. Even in species in which parental love is as strong as it is in some non-human animals and in some birds, egocentricity is also potent. In fact, egocentricity is inseparable from life; it might be said to be another name for life. A living creature is a bit of the universe which has set itself up as a kind of separate counter-universe. It tries to make the rest of the universe serve the creature's purposes and centre on the creature. That is what egocentricity means.

Of course, this is a forlorn hope. All except the most primitive species of living creatures die, and the fact of death is enough to doom egocentricity to ultimate failure; but egocentricity can never really come near to success. Non-human living creatures are unaware of the irony of their egotism. Human beings try to forget about it as much as they can, but any human being, at critical moments of his life, moments of extreme sorrow or joy or critical decision, is aware of the irony of his egocentricity, and the futility of it confronts him and distresses him. Man can deliberately combat his egocentricity, and perhaps he can partially overcome it.

All the great historic philosophies and religions have been concerned, first and foremost, with the overcoming of egocentricity. At first sight, Buddhism and Christianity and Islam and Judaism may appear to be very different from each other. But, when you look beneath the surface, you will find that all of them are addressing themselves primarily to the individual human psyche or soul; they are trying to persuade it to overcome its own self-centredness and they are offering it the means for achieving this. They all find the same remedy. They all teach that egocentricity can be conquered by love.

In the historic religions and philosophies, human examples are given of the power and the virtue of love. In the Southern form of Buddhism, especially, believers do still revere the Buddha, and some of them may try to carry out the austere, severe, difficult, spiritual exercises that the Buddha laid down for his followers;

but in the Northern form of Buddhism the Buddha plays a less important part than the bodhisattvas, and it is their example of self-sacrifice that is held up for veneration.[1] In Christianity, the same virtue of self-sacrificing love is shown not only in the story of Jesus himself but also in that of some of his followers. The example that comes first to my mind again is that of St. Francis of Assisi.

Religion will also help man in dealing with another problem which science and technology have aggravated rather than solved. I mean the problem of facing old age.

Since man is a spiritual being as well as a physical organism, and since the spiritual side of human nature is its distinctive feature, mere physical life is not, by itself, of any value for a human being. Physical life is valuable for him only in so far as it gives him an opportunity for fulfilling the spiritual purpose of human life, which is to transcend the self by loving and by following love's lead. Physical life may outlast a human being's capacity to put himself at the service of love. He may become physically incapable or spiritually incapacitated. It seems to me to be a perverse use of medical science to prolong a person's life if his life has ceased to be of value even to himself because he has outlived his capacity for contributing to and promoting the reign of love in the universe.

I have said already that science and technology have not (so far at any rate) been able to prevent the old people whom they can keep alive from becoming senile or to help them in solving other problems which beset them. Old age is at best an awkward stage of life under all social and technological conditions, and it has been made more burdensome today than ever before in countries that are technologically and medically advanced. At the very time when the physical expectation of life has been prolonged by the progress of medicine, the screw is being turned on old people on the economic plane of life. Since the close of the Second World War, mankind's income has been redistributed progressively in the more advanced countries. The workers in professions that are essential for the maintenance of our complicated modern life have been able to extract larger and larger shares by sabotaging, or by

[1] See p. 4.

merely threatening to sabotage, the functioning of the economy. The increase in their salaries, on which they have the power to insist, produces inflation and a rise of prices, and this reduces the real income of the old and the incapacitated, who are living on savings and on pensions. After all, everyone who does not die prematurely may be incapacitated during his lifetime either by sickness or by accident, and he is doomed to have to live on after having retired from working if he reaches the present average expectation of length of physical life. Non-workers cannot enforce an increase in their incomes by striking. Thus the section of the community that cannot strike effectively is being robbed by the section that can. Of course, I am not unprejudiced; I am one of the old now; but this fleecing of the helpless section of the community seems to me to be anti-social, and it is not a matter of controversy that it is also short-sighted and improvident. Inflation is not an inevitable economic malady. It is produced by the scramble for shares in the cake among those members of the community who have the power to exert pressure in order to raise their salaries.

This is a complaint made by a man of eighty-two in a Western country in the year 1971. In most times and places, there has been a three-generation family. The grandparents have lived with the children and the grandchildren all under one roof. In the future urban life, this three-generation family is unlikely to recur. On the other hand, inflation might be stopped, and thereby one present hardship of the old would be removed.

The power and wealth which are created by the application of science to technology are meaningless and valueless in face of death, and one test of a religion's worth is its attitude towards death and its efficacy or inefficacy in helping a human being to cope with the prospect of death. I have noted already that human beings appear to be unique among living creatures on this planet in being aware that they are going to die.

A dread of dying and a resentment at not being immortal have been common, though by no means universal. One of the earliest epic poems, the Sumerian epic of Gilgamesh, illustrates this. The theme is the hero's quest for immortality, and how immortality

tus was honoured for committing suicide in preference to
g senile. He felt that his mind was giving way, so he
ating and drinking and died. In the Roman world, Cato
, who was a rather foolish, unsuccessful politician, was
l for committing suicide in preference to submitting to
torship of Julius Caesar. He is named after the town in
frica, near Tunis, in which he committed suicide, so his
ade his reputation.

ue that some present-day Americans profess to take an
raeco–Roman or Asian view of suicide when they say
ead than red'. But I am not convinced that they really
I cannot see the American people preferring mass-suicide
ission to political servitude. Some people have preferred
e Carthaginians deliberately exposed themselves to the
which they suffered in 146 B.C., and their Jewish fellow
did the same in A.D. 70; but such instances of mass-suicide
and self-extermination seems to me to be foreign to the
temperament.

man being has ever been immortal on Earth so far, and
, in spite of the advance of science, it is difficult for us to
hat immortal life on Earth is one of the menaces by which
beings are threatened at present. It has, however, been
in many times and places that the souls of the dead are
n other persons in later generations, and that the series of
may recur any number of times. This is one of the tenets
is and Buddhists. It was also a tenet of at least two schools
ophy or religion in the Ancient Greek world, the Orphics
Pythagoreans.

it is noteworthy that, among people who have believed in
ty of rebirth, the dread of it has always been stronger than
d of death. In order to succeed in dying once and for all
ng thus released for ever from the 'sorrowful cycle' of
believing Buddhists and Orphics and Pythagoreans have
illing to subject themselves to strenuous spiritual and
ascetic practices.

elf do not believe in rebirth or in personal immortality
er world, either before birth or after death. I believe that

literally slips through his fingers. He has found a branch of the tree of life; it slips down into the water and a snake gets it and Gilgamesh remains mortal and dies.

At the present time, there is an extreme reluctance to face the inevitability of death among Westerners, and especially, I think, in the United States, though this shrinking from death is common to the whole Western world. For some people, of course not all people, in the United States today, death is 'unmentionable', in the sense that sexual relations were 'unmentionable' both in the United States and in other English-speaking countries in the nineteenth century. If I were drawing a caricature, I would say that death is an 'unAmerican activity', because it is still, for more simple-minded Americans, an American dogma that the United States is an earthly paradise, and inhabitants of a paradise ought to be immortal. Even the use of the word 'die' is now avoided by some Americans; they prefer to use euphemisms, such as 'pass on'. Americans risk disapproval, and even unpopularity, if they display the grief that is the natural reaction of anyone who has been bereaved by the death of someone whom he loves. This is surely perverse and unfortunate. This phobia seems to go to extremes in America, but it is characteristic of the whole of the Western world, though not, fortunately, of the whole World.

Even in Western countries this phobia about death is recent. It is no older than the advance of medical science that has lengthened the expectation of life—apart, of course, from murder in war; for science and technology, applied to armaments, have made the mass-murder of young men at an early age easier. However, science and technology, applied to medicine and surgery, have reduced the rate of other premature deaths—above all, the rate of infant mortality. A century ago, even in Western countries which were by Victorian Age standards medically advanced, death was a familiar fact of experience from an early age, and this even in well-to-do, well-fed, and medically well-cared-for families. Most people in Britain, say, a century ago, had had brothers and sisters who had died while these casualties and the survivors were still children. This experience did prevent the hard inexorable fact of death from arousing the horror and the terror that we feel for something that is unknown. In the Victorian Age, death was not unknown; it was very familiar.

Now let us look at other civilizations: for instance, the pre-Christian Greek civilization and the Indian civilization. Both of these were, and the Indian civilization still is, pessimistic about the desirability of life. The Greeks' outward actions give the impression that they had a great zest for life, yet a famous Athenian Greek poet wrote in the chorus of a play: 'The best thing of all is not to be born; but, if you have been born, the next best thing is to die young.' That is quite unlike modern Western attitudes towards death.

However, even in the West since its conversion to Christianity, there have been thinkers with the imagination and insight to perceive that interminable life in this World might be at least as unpleasant as it is to be mortal. This was pointed out very wittily and convincingly by the eighteenth-century English satirist Jonathan Swift in the account of some imaginary immortals, the Struldbrugs, which he gives in his book *Gulliver's Travels*. They live in Laputa, a 'flying saucer' hovering above Eastern Asia.

Also, the truth that human life on Earth is inevitably painful and difficult, in spite of its possible joys and pleasures, was more apparent to Westerners in the days before the progress of science and technology and rationalism had diminished physical suffering by anaesthetics and had at the same time shaken the Christian belief in immortality after death. Death at the end of a long-drawn-out painful illness used to be welcomed as a merciful release, and the brief time-span of a human life on Earth used to be regarded as an ordeal to be endured rather than as a blessing to be enjoyed. Life on Earth loomed much less large, even to nineteenth-century Westerners, than eternal life after death. Hopes and fears were concentrated on the expected afterlife rather than on the actually experienced life on Earth. A virtuous life on Earth was believed to be a passport to immortality in Heaven; a wicked life on Earth was a sentence to immortality in Hell.

Of course, life in the Western world is still painful, because the worst pains and difficulties of human life are spiritual, not physical. Surgery, anaesthetics, plumbing, and central heating cannot

diminish spiritual suffering. On the oth[...]
can be heightened by the increase of tecl[...]
can be a heavy responsibility and there[...]
ing. It is only by leaving the spiritual [...]
and by estimating the goodness or ba[...]
material terms, that the United States [...]
earthly paradise.

The present-day Western shrinking [...]
be a highly peculiar and exceptional s[...]
beings in most times and places have sp[...]
wealth on building tombs than on buil[...]
taken pleasure in making this preparat[...]
death and in dwelling on it during the [...]
valuable material objects that have be[...]
being deposited in tombs, have been t[...]
generations that has enabled modern a[...]
the material conditions of life of the p[...]
ages—and, also, by inference, their id[...]
buried with the dead by Neanderthal [...]
Pyramids and the Mausoleum and th[...]
tumulus—a real man-made mountain-[...]
in Japan.

Jews and Christians and Muslims co[...]
because they believe that it is God's pr[...]
human being should die, and that it is i[...]
a human being to decide this for him[...]
(though this has not prevented them fr[...]
the prerogative of deciding how othe[...]
them in their frequent wars). Howev[...]
well as in Eastern Asia, liberty to con[...]
person chooses has been regarded as [...]
People who perform sati or *hara-kii*[...]
heroines and as heroes; they have not [...]
as they would have been in a Chris[...]
country. This was also the attitude [...]
Old World before the conversion [...]
Roman Empire to Christianity and Isl[...]

at death a human being's soul is re-absorbed into the supra-personal spiritual presence behind the universe. I believe that personal human individuality is acquired at the price of being separated from this supra-personal reality. I feel that this price is high, and I am therefore glad that it has to be paid for a limited period only. The value of my temporary personality is, for me, two-fold. It allows me to live among other temporary personalities whom I love, and it gives me the possibility of personal achievements. But these personal achievements have value, it seems to me, only in so far as they are of some good to other people. In that case they redound 'to the glory of God'. I am here using a traditional Christian phrase for a human being's spiritual need to serve the spiritual presence behind the universe, besides serving his fellow men and women.

I have been educated both in the Christian tradition and in the pre-Christian Greek and Roman tradition. These two traditions conflict with each other. The Graeco-Roman tradition has, as I have said, much more in common with the East Asian tradition, and with the Indian too, than with the Judaic. I happen to be more Greek-minded than Judaic-minded—than Christian-minded, in other words. I do not believe in, and do not highly esteem, the Judaic conception of the nature of God. I believe that I have a human right to commit suicide if I come to the conclusion that to die now is a lesser evil for the people whom I love, and for myself, than to go on living. I regard the Jewish-Christian-Muslim ban on suicide as being an undesirable superstition. I am surprised and sorry that, in the present ex-Christian world, this Christian superstition has outlasted what seem to me to be the more valuable doctrines of Christianity. The persistent, irrational condemnation of suicide in Western countries inhibits the exercise of this human right, because it is still difficult to exercise it without shocking people whom one loves.

I have spoken several times already about my belief that, beyond all the objects which together constitute the universe, there is an ultimate spiritual presence. I want now to explain rather more fully what I mean by this spiritual presence beyond the universe and why I believe in it.

My belief is that there is an ultimate spiritual reality which gives the universe its meaning and value, and that this ultimate reality is something single, not multiple. I believe that this spiritual reality has the highest of all the claims on our love, and that, in so far as we are able to love it, it offers us guidance for determining the priorities of our love for particular objects.

My belief in this spiritual presence behind the universe is an act of faith. I cannot prove that this spiritual presence exists; I do not think that it is omnipotent; I do not know that it created the universe, or that it is this that keeps the universe going. I simply infer its existence from my direct experience of the spiritual side of human nature. Most of my fellow human beings in most times and places have made the same inference, though at different times and places they have seen the ultimate reality in different aspects, and have called it by different names: Brahmā, Nirvana, God.

Of course it is difficult to love something non-human with the fullness of love which we feel for fellow human beings, and in all the religions and philosophies there has been a tendency to personify this ultimate spiritual reality. It is easier to love the Buddha or a bodhisattva than to love Nirvana. It is easier to love the personal God Krishna than to love Brahmă, the supra-personal ultimate reality, or even than to love Brahmā, the supreme God seen as a person. It is easier to love Jesus than to love the rather remote God Yahweh, God the Father.

One of the distinctive characteristics of human nature is non-utilitarian curiosity. Human beings have an impulse to explore reality and to discover truth for their own sakes, not for any previously foreseen practical advantage for human life. For instance, human beings spent a great deal of time and energy and intellectual ingenuity on studying the stars, long before astronomy proved to be of any practical use for agriculture and for navigation. It came as a surprise when astronomy was found to be useful for knowing when to sow and reap and how to guide your ship when out of sight of land. And astronomy was studied long before any human being ever dreamed that, one day, human beings would be able to travel from our own star to other stars. I myself never dreamed, when I was a child, that I should live to see any human being reach the Moon, or that any human being ever would land on the Moon.

The motive of intellectual curiosity is non-utilitarian, but it is not disinterested. By that I mean that it is not purposeless. Curiosity that has no purpose is pointless and senseless. The purpose that inspires curiosity may not be continuously present in the inquirer's mind, and some minds may never become aware of this purpose. The underlying purpose of curiosity, whether this purpose is conscious at the moment or not, is the acquisition of knowledge and understanding for the sake of action; and the action that is the ultimate objective of human curiosity is, in my belief, action for gaining closer contact with the spiritual presence behind the universe, in order that we may enter into communion with it and bring our ephemeral selves into greater harmony with it.

Let me speak about my own experience. I am an historian. I have a curiosity about the facts of human history and about the relations between these facts. I study history simply because I have an overwhelmingly strong impulse to spend my time and my ability and my energy on the study of history. If I am asked why I do this, I say: 'I study history for fun.' As I see it, 'for fun' is another way of saying that I study history because, for me, this happens to be the avenue along which I can best find my way to communion with the ultimate reality; so 'fun' is also the most serious of all conceivable purposes.

Today, this purpose for studying something, the practice of scholarship for the purpose of seeking communion with ultimate reality, is condemned as being a vicious heresy. It is held to be unscientific to seek to acquire knowledge for any non-utilitarian ulterior motive. Research for utilitarian motives, in the sense of research for putting science to work by applying it to technology, is considered to be respectable because it produces the wealth and power which human beings want. They approve of applied science, but they do not approve of the search for knowledge when it is applied to religion, to the spiritual life of mankind. But on this issue I am an impenitent heretic. For me, the study of history would be meaningless if it did not have an ultimately religious significance and religious goal, and the motive that moves me has been, I believe, the motive for studying history that has inspired the historians of the past. I hope that it will be again the motive for the historians of the future.

I have talked a good deal about the 'morality gap', but I have not defined what I mean by morality in relation to religion. I mean by morality the standard of behaviour that is required of man, as a social being, in his relations with his fellows. In order to be in the right relation with something outside himself, a human being, as we have seen, has to overcome and transcend his own self-centredness. This is the first and the fundamental demand made on him by religion, and that is why every religion includes, among other things, a code of moral conduct. We are in more immediate and continuous contact with our human neighbours than with the presence behind the universe, so morality makes more direct and more constant demands on us in our daily life than religion makes. But the demands of morality and religion do not compete or conflict with each other. So far from that, it is difficult, if not impossible, to have the right relation either with other human beings or with the spiritual presence behind the universe if we do not have the right relation with both. Both are outside ourselves, but our lives are bound up with them. In fact, religion and morality are interdependent, and the link between them is that both require self-abnegation, self-denial, and also, if need be, self-sacrifice.

We have seen that science and technology have created a vacuum by bringing the dogmas of the higher religions into discredit, and that, in my belief, this vacuum has been filled by a return to religions of a lower kind. I ought now to explain what I mean by the terms 'higher' and 'lower' religions. By 'higher' religions I mean those that seek to put individual human beings into direct contact with ultimate spiritual reality. By 'lower' religions I mean those that seek to put individuals into indirect contact with ultimate reality through some intervening medium: either through non-human nature or through collective human power embodied in such institutions as tribes and states. I shall be discussing the 'lower' religions more fully later; let us now consider the 'higher' religions in their relation to one another.

The 'higher' religions which arose in the so-called Axis Age (I have mentioned that already) include, to my mind, Judaism, Zoroastrianism, Buddhism, Hinduism, Christianity, and Islam. The doctrines of these historic religions were formulated in social and cultural and intellectual and technological conditions that were different from ours. These doctrines are expressed in the language, not of science, but of poetry and mythology. There is a sense in which the language of poetry and mythology is timeless and is the same for all human beings and in all places, but every time and place does also have its own particular style and form of poetry and mythology, and the poetry and mythology of each higher religion are those of the particular time and place in which each of these religions happens to have arisen. Our own expressions of poetry and mythology are different, and therefore the traditional expressions of the historic religions have become partly alien to us. This is one reason why the historic religions have been losing their hold. Another reason, which I have mentioned already, is that all the established higher religions have acquired a number of non-essential accretions to which the ecclesiastical authorities sometimes cling obstinately and perversely. However, I believe that the historic higher religions all convey permanent truths, and all give counsel and offer precepts for action which are permanently valid. They all counsel us to try to overcome self-centredness and to surrender ourselves to love, and they point out practical ways of acting on this counsel. This is part of the essence of the higher religions, and it is common to them all.

We now need to disengage these permanent truths and precepts from the temporary forms that are the traditional expressions of them. We need to re-express them in forms of our own, forms which will no doubt become out of date in their turn and will have to be re-expressed again by our successors.

It is, of course, controversial to say that the permanent essence of all the higher religions is the same, and many followers of each of the different higher religions would deny this strenuously. But I think it is undoubtedly true that the ethical precepts of all the higher religions and philosophies are practically identical.

Yet I should be sorry to see the poetic and mythological

expressions of religion standardized in an entirely uniform way, though I should like to see them brought up to date. Human temperaments are not uniform, and each type of temperament needs a different form of expression for the same universally and permanently valid truths and precepts. Take Hinduism's and Islam's widely different presentations of the character of the ultimate reality behind the universe. I think these two presentations are not contrary to each other, but are complementary; they supplement each other. Hinduism conveys both the unity and the variety of ultimate reality. It dwells on the supra-personal character of ultimate reality (Brahmă), which is something more than a personality of an anthropomorphic kind, but it also presents diversity in the pantheon of Hindu gods and goddesses in human or animal form. Islam dwells on the unity of ultimate reality in its anthropomorphic facet (the aspect of it through which a human being can most easily communicate with it). It seems probable that mankind needs both presentations and that different individuals have a greater need for one of them than for the other because of their differences in temperament and outlook.

These varieties of temperament do not coincide with differences of race or nationality; they exist in every human community. What we do need is mutual tolerance between people who have different religions. We need to recognize that these different roads all lead towards an identical goal, and that there is no need to quarrel with somebody because he is following a different road. It would help to encourage this mutual tolerance if the historic religions could be liberated from their non-essential accretions, which seem to modern scientifically-orientated minds to invalidate many of the historic religions' doctrines.

I have said that, in my belief, the ethical precepts of philosophy do not differ from those of the higher religions, but I ought to make it clear that I am not referring to philosophy in the current meaning of the word. The term philosophy is now often used to mean the technical study of the workings of the conscious stratum of the human psyche, the theory of knowledge, logic, or even the analysis of the nature of language. This is really a branch of science, dealing scientifically with one facet of human nature. It is so different from philosophy in the traditional meaning of the word that we need a new word to serve as a distinctive label for this intellectual pursuit. In the original sense of the term, philosophy is hardly distinguishable from religion. Is Buddhism, for instance, a philosophy or a religion? Either word would fit it, and the same is true of most of the Ancient Greek philosophies—Stoicism and Neoplatonism, for example. Both religion and traditional philosophy are concerned with action, not only with knowledge and understanding, and both offer precepts and advice to help the individual in dealing with himself and with other people. Both are therefore concerned also with morality.

Let us now go on to consider what I call the 'lower' religions. I have said that I consider nature worship a lower form of religion because it does not bring man into direct contact with the spiritual presence behind the universe, but at the same time I do think, as I have already suggested, that man's attitude to non-human nature is of great importance and that the remnants of nature-worship which still survive in some places have a valuable contribution to make in the present-day technological and materialistic world.

Man is an integral part of nature, though he is also something more. Human nature and non-human nature have an identical relation to the spiritual presence behind the universe. For both, the meaning and value of existence is to be found in getting into harmony with the spiritual presence which is the ultimate reality. Non-human beings, of course, do this unconsciously and instinctively; human beings attempt to do it consciously and deliberately.

Primitive man had no difficulty in feeling respect for nature. Indeed, he stood in awe of nature, because he was at nature's mercy. Non-human nature was the first medium through which our ancestors, after they had awoken to consciousness, got into touch with the spiritual presence that is behind both non-human nature and human nature. Nature-worship was thus the earliest form of man's religion. The so-called nature gods are not just embodiments of nature; they are embodiments of what lies beyond nature, behind the universe; but man saw this ultimate reality through the nature at whose mercy he was.

In most parts of the World for some time past, the worship of the presence behind the universe in the form of non-human nature has been replaced either by a higher religion or by the worship of collective human power. Both these later forms of religion tend, though in different ways, to diminish man's reverence for non-human nature. They both tend to empty nature of the divine presence that really does shine through nature, though it does not originate in nature. The worship of collective human power falsely deifies man. Higher religion, at any rate in its Judaic form, its Jewish-Christian-Muslim form, pictures ultimate spiritual reality in an anthropomorphic way, in the likeness of a divine person, God; and this tempts man to think of non-human nature as having been created by God for man's use, and to feel that he is licensed to exploit nature in whatever way he may choose.

In the religious history of the Ancient Greeks, divinities that had originally stood for ultimate spiritual reality as seen through non-human nature were transformed into symbols of collective human power. For instance, the Greek goddess Athena, who had originally symbolized the cultivation of the olive-tree and the art of needlework, came to symbolize the political power of the two super-powers of the Ancient Greek world, Athens and Sparta. It is ironical that the same Athena was the city-state goddess of Athens and also the city-state goddess of Sparta—the same goddess for two rival powers. Of course, there had been nothing incongruous in their having the same goddess of olive-cultivation and art in the days before Athena had been 'politicized'.

I believe that, in Japan, Shinto, which is the worship of the ultimate reality through non-human nature, was politicized in the same way, temporarily, after the Meiji Revolution in 1868. But, since the end of the Second World War, Shinto has been purged— if I have got the facts right—of this political perversion and has been given back its original function of putting man into touch with ultimate spiritual reality through non-human nature. If I am correctly informed about this, Japan is fortunate in still possessing in Shinto the worship of ultimate reality through non-human nature in the original form of this religion.

In our time, man has been violating and desecrating non-human nature all over the World. In Japan, it is my impression that the obliteration of man's original natural environment by an artificial, man-made environment has now been carried to further extremes than anywhere else so far. Shinto is surely a precious antidote to this. In those parts of the World in which the Judaic conception of the character of ultimate reality has prevailed, the equivalents of Shinto, which were once living realities there too, have long ago been extinguished.

However, even in the theistic-minded and technological-minded Western world, there have been a few religious and poetic geniuses who have retained or who have revived primitive man's reverence for nature as a manifestation of the spiritual presence behind the universe. I have already quoted a poem of St. Francis of Assisi's in praise of God as the creator of inanimate nature and of all living things. I think there is a message for the present-day Western world, indeed for the whole present generation of mankind, in St. Francis's hymn, and in the poem of the Pantheistic English poet Wordsworth which he called 'Intimations of Immortality'. I do not know whether Wordsworth was consciously aware of the quest for Nirvana, but, as I see it, it is the Buddhist's conception of Nirvana, not the Christian's conception of immortality, that Wordsworth is describing and that he is seeking to recapture in this poem.

When I visit the sacred precinct at Ise in Japan, the central shrine of Shinto, I feel that here the form of religion which St. Francis and Wordsworth were trying to bring back to life is still fully alive. The spirit with which the visitor to Ise finds himself in contact is a spirit that the present generation throughout the world needs to cultivate in order to dissuade nature from taking her revenge for the impious violence that modern man has done to her.

In India, respect for non-human nature has been carried even further than in Japan, though here it takes the form of respect for non-human living creatures rather than of an emotional relation with inanimate nature. Birds and animals are not frightened of human beings in India. Hawks and kites will come within a few feet of you. Cows will lie down in the road in front of your car and will feel sure that they will not be run over. And one Indian sect, the Jain sect, which I have mentioned already, excels in its reverence and considerateness for non-human life. Mahavira, the founder of Jainism, was a contemporary of the Buddha, but Jainism has stayed in India, whereas Buddhism has spread all over the world. The Jains carry their respect for life to such lengths that they will not kill even mosquitoes, and they put cloths over their mouths in order to avoid swallowing insects by accident. This may seem to Westerners to be going too far; but there is beauty and value in it, and I think the modern world would do well to learn something from the Jain religion of India as well as from the Shinto religion of Japan.

When man got the upper hand over non-human nature, he took, at most times and in most places, to worshipping his own collective power instead of worshipping nature. The worship of collective power did meet man's need for dealing with his self-centredness by getting out of himself, but at the price of enslaving his soul by telling him to love nothing beyond his own tribe's power. To my mind this is an evil form of religion. In Christian, Jewish, and Islamic terms, it is a form of idolatry. The transfer of man's worship from nature to his own collective power seems to me to be a great spiritual regression.

In this second form of what I call the 'lower' religions, the human community is made virtually into a god, and it may try to persuade or compel its subjects to become accomplices in immoral behaviour—for instance in fighting aggressive wars and in committing atrocities. In any case, no human community can be a permanent object of worship, since all are likely to be short-lived. Take the Kingdom of Prussia, for instance. The Kingdom of Prussia had a dramatic rise in the eighteenth and nineteenth centuries and came to an equally dramatic sudden end in 1945. It is most unlikely that Prussia will ever come into existence again; and this is typical of the history of states. Some states have been much longer-lived than Prussia—for instance, China, the Japanese Empire, Cambodia, Sweden—but, compared to the length of human history, every state, like every other human institution, is relatively short-lived. Yet this deification of human power requires the devotees of a deified state to sacrifice their lives, and perhaps their honour also, for the sake of this idol. States are not really gods, they are public utilities, like roads and bridges and electricity and water and gas.

Yet, in my belief, the worship of the collective power of a fraction of the human race at the expense of the rest of the human race—nationalism, in other words—is the real religion today of a majority of people. Nationalism has been superseded only nominally by the 'higher' religions, each of which aims at converting the whole of mankind to its own prescription for putting the individual into touch with ultimate reality. Whether we profess to be followers of one of the historic higher religions or not, almost all of us are nationalists under the skin.

Nationalism has been the ruin of one civilization after another, beginning with the earliest of them all, the Sumerian. City-states evoke a more fanatical loyalty than national states, and the Sumerian world, like the Ancient Greek world, was a world of city-states. This loyalty to local states, whatever their scale, produces international conflicts, and these become intolerable. In most of the previous cases, nationalism has eventually been suppressed by the forcible imposition of a world state or would-be world state. But this drastic remedy has usually been applied too late to save from dissolution a society on which the religion of nationalism has already inflicted mortal wounds.

In our time, nationalism has become increasingly fanatical and has been infecting smaller and smaller fractions of the world's population. Today the Indian Union, which used to be bound together by the Hindu religion and way of life, has been threatened with a break-up by the rise in India of a local linguistic nationalism of the East European type. Since Independence, India has been re-mapped on linguistic lines, and there are now in India all those disputes about areas of mixed population, and about boundary lines between language-areas, that we find in Europe. In Britain, Scottish and Welsh nationalism is now asserting itself against English nationalism. Since the end of the Second World War the number of sovereign independent national states on the land surface of this planet has more than doubled. I think there were less than seventy at the outbreak of the Second World War, and there are now 140 at least.

The last two centuries have seen the break-up of a number of regional empires: first the Spanish Empire, which broke up in the early nineteenth century, then the Turkish, in the course of the nineteenth century, then the Austrian, at the end of the First World War, then the Japanese, at the end of the Second World War, and finally the British, the French, and the Dutch, after the Second World War. So the human race has been split up into an ever larger number of ever smaller-sized political units.

This centrifugal tendency on the political plane is running directly counter to the contemporary centripetal tendency on the technological plane. I believe that in the present-day world technology is a still more potent force than nationalism. I therefore expect that the World is going to be united politically in the teeth of nationalistic resistance. In the atomic age the World cannot be united by military conquest, which was the traditional method of political unification in the past. I fear, though, that it is likely to be united in the first instance by a world-wide union of the rich minority for the immoral purpose of trying to hold down the poor majority.

At present we have a balance of terror, a balance of deterrents between national states, and we all know how very fragile, how unstable and insecure, this way of preserving peace is. In fact, it cannot be durable. How, then, can we arrive at a true, and therefore lasting, peace? I do not believe that this goal can be reached without a world-wide spiritual revolution. Certainly a reformation of mankind's political organization would be required. The people of each local sovereign state will have to renounce their state's sovereignty and subordinate it to the paramount sovereignty of a literally world-wide world government. But this revolution in mankind's political organization can be brought about only as a consequence of a far more radical and more profound revolution, a revolution in our fundamental ideas and ideals. For a true and lasting peace, a religious revolution is, I am sure, a *sine qua non*. By religion, as I hope I have made clear, I mean the overcoming of self-centredness, in both individuals and communities, by getting into communion with the spiritual presence behind the universe and by bringing our wills into harmony with it. I think this is the only key to peace, but we are very far from picking up this key and using it, and, until we do, the survival of the human race will continue to be in doubt.

5
Education: A Means of Constructive Change

WAKAIZUMI: The basic concepts of education as well as the resources at its disposal are in a rapid state of transformation. How will this affect the many roles that education must play in society?

Education implies transmission, and transmission implies reciprocal action between two parties. In the transmission of a cultural heritage, the parties are the rising generation and its elders. To what extent does the rising generation need its elders' help for finding its feet? And are there limits to the help that the older generation can give, even supposing that the younger generation is in the mood for being receptive? How far, if at all, can we learn at second hand from our predecessors' experience? To what extent is human nature capable of adapting itself to new circumstances for which its education has not prepared it? In our time, the technological gap between East and West seems to be creating serious dislocations in many countries of the World. Can education help to rectify these dislocations? Can education be fortified by the very technology which seems to be at fault? How will education be used? In a time of rapid change, can Utopian ideas help mankind to survive the future? Can we find a practical form of education for people in general?

Up to this point, I have been raising questions that are, I think, relevant to education in all times and places, but some of the educational questions that are most hotly debated today are perhaps peculiar to our own time. What are the pros and cons of specialization in a society in which the quantities and magnitudes of so many elements in man's environment have been increasing enormously? Considering the diversity of people's natural gifts, and also the variety in the degree of their ability, how far should education be diverse and selective, and how far should it be uniform and egalitarian? At the university level, is teaching compatible, under present conditions, with doing creative work? Can education help people to find a satisfactory and valuable use for the leisure that is going to be imposed on them by automation? Can education help the peoples of the World to unite into a single world-wide society?

TOYNBEE: How can the older and the younger generation rise to the present difficult and critical occasion and bridge the gap between them? As always in all human relations, through mutual love and through a recognition, by each individual, of the inadequacy of his own love. If he faces this truth about himself, he will feel humility, contrition, and compassion. He will think less of his own troubles and grievances and will think more of the other party's.

In this field, all human beings are on an equal footing. The young and the old are confronted by the same spiritual challenge, and they have the same capacity, and therefore the same obligation, to respond to this common human challenge with all their might. But there is another field—the field of experience—in which, owing to the accident of their difference in age, they are not on a par with each other. The older generation has had a longer and fuller experience of life than the rising generation. The experience of *karma* is part of what the older generation has learnt, and it has an obligation to pass on the fruits of its experience, including the whole of the social and cultural heritage from its own predecessors. This is what we mean by education in the broadest sense of the word, and, in the nature of the case, education cannot be reciprocal to more than a limited extent. The young can reject education, but they can hardly give it. In the main, therefore, education means help from the parents' generation for the children's generation. Of course, we all also have to learn to help and save ourselves, but, in a social species such as man is, the help for learning can and should be given largely by the older generation.

I was going to say that education is something specifically human, but this is not quite true. For instance, I have seen father and mother birds educating a young bird to fly. However, for practical purposes, education is a specifically human characteristic, because most species of living creatures have their lives governed by built-in instincts; and these instincts are transmitted from one generation to another by physical procreation, and, being transmitted in that way, they cannot be changed by acts of will. Apparently instincts can be changed only by physical mutations in the genes. It is not yet in our power to modify genes by direct human planned action. We may be able to do that one day, but at present we cannot do it. So, if man depended for his development solely on his genes, he would have to wait as long as non-human creatures have to wait. But mankind seems to be unique in having its life governed only to a minor extent by natural instincts which change only when there are physical mutations in the transmitted genes. Mankind's life is governed to a major extent by man-made institutions which are transmitted from one generation to another, not through physical procreation, but through education. This process of transmitting a social and cultural heritage is carried out, not only by schoolmasters and schoolmistresses, but by parents and by all the other members of the older generation with whom a member of the rising generation comes into contact.

A culture changes far more rapidly than a set of instincts. A culture changes even when both the transmitting and the receiving generation are doing their utmost to preserve the tradition unchanged and intact. Take the case of language. Language changes rapidly and irresistibly, even when the members of society are trying to keep a language 'frozen' in some form that the community has treasured as being classical. There was a form of Latin, for instance, that was stamped as being 'classical', and for centuries people tried to go on writing and talking this Latin, even when they were actually writing and talking French, Italian, Spanish, Romanian, and other Romance languages. They could not keep the language fixed, and what is true of language is true of culture in general.

Institutions can be changed both rapidly and radically when a change is desired by the transmitting generation or by the receiving generation or by both. There have been quite a number of deliberate educational revolutions, some of them extorted by the young, some imposed by the older generation, while some (and this is the happiest way) have been made by agreement between the older generation and the rising generation.

We need now to re-examine scholarship and education, as they have been traditionally thought of, in the light of the very rapid changes in our society, in our way of life, in our values, and in our systems of thought and our institutions.

Many people now believe that the present need for mass-education can be met to a large extent by an increased use of the television screen for educational purposes, and I should like to say a few words about this now, though I shall be dealing later with what seem to me to be the effects of television viewing on society in general.

In illiterate societies, pictures have always been used to serve the purpose that script serves in literate societies. Temples and churches have always been decorated with pictures and statues because an illiterate person can understand the meaning of, say, stories from the Bible if they are presented to him in this form, and especially if they are interpreted for him by a priest. In much the same way, television can play a useful part now in undeveloped countries where a large proportion of the population cannot read. It can be used, for instance, to show backward peoples new agricultural techniques and principles of public health. I have no doubt, also, that television can be used beneficially in developed countries to supplement the traditional methods of instruction of the large numbers of students who now throng to our schools and universities. I believe that an increasing use is being made of television for this purpose in the United States, for instance, and, if I am correctly informed, it is found to be particularly valuable in imparting knowledge of various branches of science.

But the frequent viewing of non-educational television pictures by children does seem to me to be dangerous, and to have a definitely non-educative effect, because it blurs the distinction between make-believe and reality. A child watches a 'Western' on television, and he knows that this is make-believe; he knows that he is seeing actors dressed as cowboys pretending to shoot each other. But in a moment or two there will appear a picture from real life—say, a battle or a massacre in Vietnam—in which people are really killing and wounding each other. How is the child to distinguish between the make-believe picture on the television screen and the realities of life? May he not be inclined to regard everything that happens in the world as being, in a sense, make-believe about which he is not called upon to take any action?

I received my education long before the days of television and I have been an inveterate reader ever since, so I am not without bias on this question. But it does seem to me that, compared with reading, television viewing is a passive activity, hostile to the principle of 'do-it-yourself'. But 'do-it-yourself' is the essence of education. The aim of all education is, or should be, to teach people to educate themselves, whether they want to engage in some intellectual activity or in some practical, technological kind of activity. Before the days of television, a publishing firm could be, as it generally still is, a much smaller affair than a television organization, and the hundreds of thousands of books that are produced by publishing firms give the reader a far greater choice than the viewer has. The viewer has to sit passively watching what the directors of the relatively small number of television networks choose to put before him; he has much less freedom of choice than the reader. Before the invention of books, oral communication gave an even wider freedom of choice, since any topic could be discussed in the course of conversation. In an Ancient Greek city-state or in a medieval Italian city-state, the talker in the agora or piazza could and did discuss freely any subject in which he and his fellow citizens were interested. They were not passive; they were 'doing it themselves'. Oral communication, in the form of lectures and disputations, also played a larger part than reading and writing in medieval Western universities.

We are going through a time of extreme change, and we have to ask ourselves whether past precedents are any guide to the future. Can predictions based on the past any longer be valid? Can we learn from experience? It has been suggested that society may be entering now into a phase of discontinuity because of the transformation of the World by technology. We have to ask ourselves whether this change has made all past history irrelevant to the future. We have also to ask ourselves whether history has ever really repeated itself in the past.

We have to ask this because the Hindus and the Ancient Greeks, for instance, believed that history does repeat itself. In the Hindu and Ancient Greek view, this repetition is necessary and inexorable. The Ancient Chinese did not believe that repetition is inevitable, but they did believe that repetition ought to be brought about as far as possible by deliberate human effort. They believed this because, in the Chinese view, the conduct and the precepts of the Founding Fathers of the Chinese civilization were models that were of unsurpassable excellence and that therefore they ought to be imitated for ever. It was possible, the Chinese held, to depart from these models, but this always produced disasters.

The Israelites, followed on this point by the Christians and the Muslims, held quite a different view. The Israelites, and their successors the Jews, the Christians, and the Muslims, believed that history is non-repetitive because they believed that history is planned by God, and that God's will is unchanging and omnipotent. Since, on this Judaic view, the planning of history is not the work of human wills that might frustrate each other, the course of human history is preordained from start to finish, that is to say from the creation of the universe by God to God's Last Judgement on the human race, alive or dead. The partial freedom of human wills is not denied in this view, but, even if human wills were all to concur with each other in opposing God's plan, human wills would not be able to prevail against God's will. The most that they would be able to do would be to postpone the fulfilment of God's will, and even this only if God acquiesced.

Logically, the Jewish-Christian-Muslim vision of history as moving in a straight line towards an objective is irreconcilable with the vision of history as moving repeatedly round a fixed circular track, which is the Ancient Indian and Ancient Greek view. Actually, movements of both these logically irreconcilable kinds can be discerned, I think, in man's history.

When I look back on the past course of human history, I believe that I am not mistaken in detecting in it a certain amount of pattern in the shape of regularities and uniformities and recurrences. For instance, a number of past societies—not only the Greek but the Sumerian society and the Chinese society too—have been divided up politically into a number of small local sovereign states at the start, when the curtain rings up on the play and we get the earliest glimpse of their history. These local states have then gone to war with each other repeatedly; the wars have grown more violent and more destructive; and eventually peace has been purchased at the price of submission to a world state, or a partial world state, like the Roman Empire, the Akkadian Empire in the case of the Sumerians, and the Chinese Empire. In these instances history has taken the form of what one might call a set of plays, each play revealing the same fundamental plot beneath the superficial differences between one play and another. The resemblance, in fact, between the structures of Greek history, Sumerian history, and Chinese history is striking. As I see them, there is a genuine pattern common to all three of them.

How is the historical fact of pattern compatible with the reality of freedom of choice? I do believe that human beings have a certain amount of freedom of choice, but they can and do forfeit their freedom by falling into conflicts with each other in which their opposing wills frustrate each other and cancel each other out. The nemesis of discord is then the loss of freedom of action. Human affairs fall out of control. Instead of being planned to fulfil unpredictable human wishes, human affairs now follow natural laws, like those that govern non-human affairs. And natural law means regularity, recurrence, and repetition. I think that, even when human control over human affairs is lost, the future does not become predictable, but some guesses about the future then do become more probable than others in the light of the patterns that are discernible in the course of past events.

I think it is certainly possible to learn from past experience. The cultural heritage that is transmitted from one generation to another by education includes memories of outstanding past events. The repertory of a society's collective memory contains records of the consequences, satisfactory or unsatisfactory, of past actions, past attitudes of mind, past ideals or lack of ideals. We do have the requisite information for recognizing and avoiding past mistakes and for recognizing and emulating past successes, if we can make the effort to behave rationally. But we seldom do make this effort until we have been goaded into it by suffering.

Human nature has a strong emotional and impulsive element in it. So far, we have usually proved not to be rational enough to profit by other people's experience to anything like the extent that our records of this past experience put within our power. This is true of individuals. How far have any of us been willing to profit by our parents' experience? And how successful have our parents been in enabling their children to profit by their experience? A lot of human experience spills over to waste, because children, like all human beings, are stiff-necked and are unwilling to take things on trust from other people. They therefore have to learn all over again by their own hard experience; and what is true of individuals is equally true of communities. In our collective behaviour we are all as prone as young people are to ignore the lessons of past experience.

I think my own countrymen, the English, have perhaps been unusual in taking to heart the lessons of past national mistakes. I will give three instances of this.

First of all, Joan of Arc cured the English of their medieval ambition to make conquests on the Continent. In the eleventh century a continental power, Normandy, had conquered Britain, and, as a result, Britain had come to be linked politically, for a century and a half, with considerable parts of France. When the English Crown lost those French possessions, the English tried again and again to reconquer parts of France. Since our experience with Joan of Arc, we have never tried to do that again.

Secondly, England was the first West European country in modern times to make a violent anti-monarchical revolution. In the seventeenth century we waged a civil war, and the victors in that war cut off the King's head. The consequence was a military dictatorship. Cromwell divided the country up into a number of military districts, each of them under a major-general, and the English did not like that. So, after Cromwell's death, they quickly re-established the monarchy, though now with only limited powers. When Charles I's second successor, his son, James II, seemed to be trying to revert to absolutism, the English deposed him, but they took great care not to put him to death. He was running away and a fisherman caught him and handed him over to the Government, expecting that he would get a reward. What he got was a scolding, and the Government shut their eyes while James II ran away again, this time to safety. He was a nuisance as an exile, but as a martyr, like his father Charles I, he would have been far more of a nuisance, and the English had learned enough by then to realize this.

Thirdly, the English lost their North American colonies by refusing to give them the amount of self-government for which they asked. Since then, we have usually taken care to give independence to other parts of the former British Empire—for instance, to Canada, Australia, India, Pakistan, Malaya—before they have seized independence by force, and our rather humiliating eviction from Cyprus and from Aden in recent years shows that we had learned the right lesson and that, when we did not act on our lesson, we were courting the defeat and humiliation that we had suffered in North America in the eighteenth century.

Of course, other peoples have learned lessons from history too. France's four defeats in 1713, 1814, 1815 (two years running), and 1871 seem to have cured France of the ambition to dominate Europe by military force, and I believe that the defeats of 1918 and 1945 have had a similar effect on Germany. I think Japan has learned from the shock of being not only defeated in 1945 but being then occupied by a foreign power for the first time in Japanese history. The Mongols failed, in two attempts, to gain even a beach-head in Japan, yet the Mongol Empire was the biggest empire that the World has ever seen so far. I fancy that the Japanese took the lesson of 1945 to heart all the more poignantly because Japan's unprecedentedly disastrous defeat in 1945 had followed close on the heels of her very sensational victories in the earlier stages of the Second World War, and these victories had followed on her victories over China in 1894 and over Russia in 1904–5. Japan had been winning an unbroken series of victories, and then suddenly her gains were all taken away in a shattering defeat. I am sure that this experience has entered deep into Japanese minds and hearts.

These examples show that nations are capable of learning lessons from history and that they have sometimes acted on these lessons. However, there are probably many more cases of invincible blindness to the lessons of experience; and, though it is true that both France and Germany have been cured of military ambitions in the end, it took France four and Germany two great defeats before the country learned the lesson which the first of these defeats might have taught her.

Almost every section of the human race is now experiencing radical changes in its way of life, its institutions, its ideals. The principal cause of this is the shock that has been given to our traditional views and habits by the impact of the science and technology that have been brought into existence in the Western society within the last three centuries and that have now affected all the World. The force of this impact is so great that it is now upsetting even the Western society which gave birth to science and technology of the modern kind, and the impact must be much more upsetting for other societies which imported science and technology (a rather exotic import in some cases). One of the lessons that we can learn from experience is that it is possible to adapt to rapid changes in the environment, including those that have been brought about by technological development. In another connection, I have already mentioned the earliest instance known to us. About 30,000 years ago a portion of mankind invented, relatively suddenly, the new and improved pattern of tools that was worked out by Upper Palaeolithic man. I think that this change in their tools must have given our primitive ancestors a psychological shock comparable to the shock given to their eighteenth-century descendants by the Industrial Revolution in Britain.

Moreover, it is not only technological developments that have given shocks and have required adaptation. The same challenge has been presented by the impact of foreign cultures—including, of course, foreign religions, since religion is an important aspect of culture. There have been impacts of foreign cultures in which a new technology was only a part, and not the most important part, of the total new combination of foreign elements with which people suddenly had to cope.

I should like to start illustrating this point by examples from Japanese history. In the sixth century of the Christian era three foreign civilizations were all simultaneously impinging on Japan when the Indian religion of Buddhism made its impact on the Japanese in its Chinese and Korean form. Then, in the next century, the seventh century of the Christian era, Japan had to meet the impacts of the political system of the T'ang dynasty and of the

cultural basis of this system, the Confucian code of conduct and
method of education on which the Chinese imperial régime
depended. Then, in the sixteenth and seventeenth centuries, the
Western civilization made its impact on Japan. On the previous
occasions, Japan had opened herself to Buddhism and to Chinese
culture, but, after her first experience of the Western culture, she
rejected it and expelled the Westerners.

But there was a fourth impact. In the nineteenth century the
West made an impact on Japan again with all the massive power
that had been given to the West by the Industrial Revolution. This
time Japan realized that she must come to terms with this industrialized West, and she also realized that technology was only one
element in the Western culture and that, if she adopted Western
technology—for instance, Western weapons—she must adopt
many other Western things as well.

I could illustrate my present point just as well from Russian
history. In the ninth and tenth centuries there was an impact on
Russia of Christianity in its Eastern Orthodox form and of the
medieval Greek culture, the Byzantine culture. In this case, as in
the impact of India and China on Japan, the technological element
was relatively minor; yet, of all the foreign impacts on Russia so
far, I am convinced that the first in the series, the impact of Greek
Christianity, has been by far the most profound and the most
enduring. You cannot understand Lenin—a man who had been
brought up as an Eastern Orthodox Christian—unless you understand Lenin's Byzantine background.

At the end of the seventeenth century the Western post-
Christian world, not this time the Greek Christian world, made an
impact on Russia, and this time technology was more important.
The West was then beginning to apply science to technology and
therefore to forge ahead of the rest of the World in technology.
Fortunately for Russia, however, she had at that moment as her
autocrat Peter the Great, who was a born technician. Peter loved
doing things with his hands; he worked in shipbuilding yards in
Holland and in Britain. Peter the Great forced the Western technology of his day on Russia and so saved her from being conquered by her Western neighbours. But, in Peter the Great's

time, technology was not the only thing that Russia borrowed from the West. She borrowed the so-called modern 'enlightenment', the religious toleration, the rational way of looking at the universe, the science, in other words, of the late seventeenth and early eighteenth centuries in the West. And then again in the twentieth century there was an impact on Russia of the post-Industrial Revolution Western way of life. This made its impact in the Communist form—a Western ideology which is a protest against, and a rejection of, the Western way of life as this has taken shape in the West itself.

In both these later cases, ideology, as well as technology, has been important, and it was the ideological revolution that gave the stimulus to the technological revolution, anyway in the case of the Communist revolution in Russia. Lenin made the Communist revolution first, and then he said: 'Socialism means electricity'. In order to preserve the Communist revolution in Russia, Lenin had to modernize Russian technology.

I could go further. I could refer to the impact of Western military technology on Turkey in the eighteenth and nineteenth centuries, and to the total reception of the Western civilization in the twentieth century, which was imposed on Turkey by the dictatorial methods of Mustafa Kemal Atatürk. I could discuss the military and intellectual and artistic impact of the Ancient Greek civilization on Ancient Egypt and South-West Asia in and after the time of Alexander the Great. There was also a religious counter-impact of other parts of the world on the Graeco-Roman world in the form of the Judaic religions of Christianity and Islam.

One form which an attempt to profit from the lessons of experience has sometimes taken has been the imagining of Utopian societies. This started in Ancient Greece, and it is to be noted that the Greeks started to write accounts of imaginary ideal societies after, and because, they felt that their civilization had passed its peak. Ancient Greek Utopias were blue-prints of projects for arresting and reversing the decline of civilization by re-elevating it to the level of its past zenith. Short of that, these Greek Utopias were projects for pegging civilization at its present level in the hope of saving it from sinking still lower. The Greek Utopias

were therefore backward-looking and conservative and reactionary. This is true especially of the Athenian philosopher Plato. The
most famous of his dialogues, in which he sketches an imaginary
society, is *The Republic*, but in his old age he wrote a still longer
dialogue called *The Laws*. The imaginary society described in
The Laws is more down-to-earth than the society in *The Republic*,
and it is also more reactionary, socially and politically. It is, in
fact, a fascist society, or you might say a medieval Christian society
in which heretics are put to death if they refuse to confess and
recant their heretical errors. It is strange to find this in Ancient
Greece in the pre-Christian Age.

The imaginary society described in
These Ancient Greek Utopias express a conscious and deliberate
opposition to the tendency of Greek history at the dates at which
the successive Utopias were composed. Therefore it is not surprising that these Utopias had no practical effect on the course of
Greek history, and that their blue-prints bear no relation to what
actually happened. The Greek Utopias all sought to rehabilitate
the sovereign city-state. Plato and Aristotle ignored what was
happening under their eyes. What actually happened was that the
city-states ruined themselves by fighting war after war with each
other, until finally they were all incorporated in, and subordinated
to, a single world state, the Roman Empire, which gave them
peace at the cost of taking away their sovereign independence.

In the Western world at the Renaissance a fresh crop of Utopias
was produced. These modern Western Utopias were inspired by
the Greek patterns; they took the same general form as Plato's
and Aristotle's imaginary societies; but their purpose was not the
same. The age in which these early modern Western Utopias were
composed was an age of optimism, not of pessimism. These are
not blue-prints for recapturing the past; they are projects for
breaking away from the past in the hope of creating a future that
will be different in the sense of being better. The very word
'Utopia' was not invented by the Ancient Greeks themselves;
it was unknown to them, though it is an artificial Greek word. 'U'
means 'not', 'topos' means 'place'. 'Utopia' means 'not a place', 'a
place that is nowhere', an imaginary place.

The sixteenth-century English scholar St. Thomas More's Utopia is sited somewhere in the New World, which, in his time, had just been discovered. This is interesting, because some present-day Americans still cling to the belief that they have discovered, or have built up, an earthly paradise, a kind of Utopia, on the North American continent. It is not by accident that More places his Utopia outside the Old World, of which his own country, England, was a part.

The present age is an age of uncertainty and apprehension. We do not feel that a return to the past is either possible or desirable, but we also do not see our way into the future. In our time the World is changing so rapidly and in such unforeseen ways that it is not surprising that, at present, the invention of Utopias is felt to be futile. There have been some satirical Utopias, George Orwell's *1984*, and Aldous Huxley's *Brave New World*; but serious Utopias have been rather rare in our generation. However, I think there is a real possibility that, in the next chapter of the World's history, we may be going to purchase survival at the price of submitting to an authoritarian world government (I shall be dealing with this possibility later); and, if I am right about this, I daresay that one of the propaganda devices that the coming world tyranny might use, in the hope of reducing this régime's unpopularity, would be to commission the writing of Utopias drawing idealized pictures of past attempts at establishing something like world governments— such attempts as the Persian Empire, the Roman Empire, and the Chinese Empire.

I have discussed earlier the 'morality gap' and I have mentioned the 'credibility gap'. Now I am going to take up what might be called the 'scholarship gap', which has been created by the modern tendency towards specialization.

It is true that in the past, both in China and in the West, a 'humane' education did involve an undesirable degree of specialization, because it concentrated on the study of a set of works of literature that had been canonized as being 'classical'. I myself had as thorough a grounding in the Greek and Latin Classics as my Chinese contemporaries had in the Confucian 'classics'. (In China, the competitive examination in the classics for candidates for the civil service was discontinued in 1905. In Britain, the civil service

examiners continued to give an excessive reward to proficiency in
the Greek and Latin classics down to 1914, if not till a later date.)
But a truly humane education need not be, and should not be,
exclusively, or even mainly, 'classical'. It should include a study of
all the greatest works of literature that the human race has produced so far (students will have to study most of these in translation). It should also include a study of the visual arts and music,
which can reach all eyes and ears without being checked by the
barrier of differences of language. Above all, a humane education
should include a study of all the higher religions and philosophies.

At the present time, however, the tendency is towards a far
higher degree of specialization than was ever involved in the old-
fashioned Chinese or Western 'classical' education. Why do people
specialize so minutely nowadays, and what problems does specialization create? This is a rather personal question for me, because I
have been involved, unexpectedly and reluctantly, in a certain
amount of controversy over this, as a result of my own work.

The present tendency towards aimless learning and the specialization for which it opens the way is not peculiar to scholarship;
in the present-day world, specialization is characteristic of all kinds
of activity. The so-called 'Zeitgeist', to use a useful German word,
is very pervasive nowadays all over the World, and this makes it all
the more difficult to check and overcome specialization.

In scholarship, I am very conscious of the tendency towards
specialization—I would say towards over-specialization (I am
showing my colours; what I have just said is controversial)—
because I myself am a deliberate and determined generalist. I have
encountered a certain amount of intolerance on the part of some
specialists, which has surprised me by its violence, and by even, in
some cases, what has appeared to be almost a personal animosity.
Animosity over moral or political questions seems to me to be
unfortunate, misguided, and deplorable, but animosity over intellectual questions strikes me as being ludicrous. I do not feel
counter-animosity against people who differ from me on this
question.

The cause of specialization is, of course, obvious. The number of
things that there are to be known nowadays has increased so

greatly, and the intricacy and the complicatedness of all these things has also so much increased, that there is a strong temptation to try to retain a mastery over knowledge and action by breaking up the field of action and the field of knowledge into smaller and smaller patches. The feeling is: if only I can reduce it to this tiny patch, perhaps I can master it, however full of detail it may be. But I myself believe that this is not a true solution of a problem that, no doubt, is genuine and formidable.

I think that it is not the true solution because, when a field of either knowledge or action is insulated from its setting, from its environment, this insulation is artificial and arbitrary, and therefore the attempt to study or to take action about reality within these narrow limits is bound to miscarry. Our vision of reality is distorted when we do not see each patch in its general setting; so the specialist who sees the part and not the whole does not see correctly. His view is put out of focus by being narrowed down. What is equally serious, the specialist in action does not act right, because he is acting on behalf of the part only and not the whole of the universe.

For instance, the foreign minister of one of about 140 separate states is often acting for his fraction of the human race as against all other fractions. He may act very immorally in the narrow interests of his own little country—and every country is little compared to the whole human race. To take another example, a trustee's business in private life is to look after the interests of the person for whom he is administering a trust, and not to look after the interests of humanity. He takes a narrow view of his obligations, and often his actions are, I should say, misguided and anti-moral for this reason. We can only act really well, only see really clearly, if we act for the good of the whole and if we see the whole and what lies behind the whole of the universe.

Now we come back to the realm of scholarship, which is my concern at this point, and not the realm of action. If we were to reach a state of affairs in which specialists studied and wrote exclusively for their fellow specialists in the same field, scholarship would be discredited because it would be reduced to absurdity.

Creative work will be barren if it does not produce some

valuable social effect. The thinker, artist, poet, and prophet must have a public. In the prophet's case, this is obvious; but it is also true in other forms of creative work that the worker must give the fruits of his work to his fellow human beings in some form. If he works only for himself or only for a tiny clique of fellow specialists, his career will have been a social failure and probably a professional failure too. In any case, exhaustive knowledge is unattainable even if it is pursued by resorting to an extreme degree of specialization.

I had an old friend who decided that he would write the history of the English Parliament. He came from another country, so he was particularly interested in this strange English institution. He decided to work in a very concrete way, by studying the individual careers of Members of Parliament. In the end he got down to studying twenty years of parliamentary history, then one year, then a few months. He did study the biographies of a considerable number of Members of Parliament over a certain number of years, but he never managed to record what these members did, what legislation they passed and what they did not pass, and the effect of their activities on the fortunes of Britain and of the World while they were Members of Parliament. He lost his way among the trees and he never saw the whole wood.

I think that here the discovery, in my lifetime, of the subconscious level of the human psyche has a lesson for us. Freud and Jung and their successors have shown us that, in the smallest fraction of time of which it is possible for the human mind to become conscious, the amount of actions and events that take place in the psyche is virtually infinite. The Irish writer, James Joyce, in his book *Ulysses*, attempted to set down a number of psychic actions that took place within the souls of half a dozen men and women who are the characters in his book during one period of twenty-four hours. Joyce wrote a very big book, but he himself would have agreed that the amount of his characters' psychic action that he was able to express on paper is only a minute fraction of what actually would have passed if these fictitious characters had been real persons. What I am getting at is that the goal of exhaustive knowledge, even about what happens in the smallest period of time, is unattainable. It is a will o' the wisp; its pursuit is a wild goose chase.

As I see it, a scholar's public ought not to be limited to his fellow specialists. He ought to produce work that is intelligible and valuable for the non-specialist cultivated intelligent public. This is his social and cultural duty.

In simpler and smaller societies—for instance, in Japan before the introduction of Buddhism and of Chinese civilization, or in Britain before the introduction of Christianity—every member of society could do and could know practically everything that there was to be done and to be known. It was the same in Iceland before the introduction of Christianity there about the year 1000. In larger and more complex societies, each of us has to be a specialist to some extent.

Generalism is always indispensable; but, in a society in which there is a great deal of ground to be covered, generalism too has its dangers. The specialist's vision will become distorted, but the generalist's vision may become superficial, as the specialist often points out. I think the safeguard against both these dangers is to combine specialism in some particular field with a general knowledge of the rest of the field. A patch of specialism will keep the generalist up to standard, and a touch of generalism will save the specialist's vision from falling out of focus. Generalism and specialism can be combined in many different proportions. Each scholar must follow his own bent in finding the proportions that suit his personal intellectual make-up. What he must take care to avoid is becoming either a specialist or a generalist exclusively.

It seems to me that excessive specialization is one of the most serious obstacles in our way if we want, as we do, to make education in the broader sense (including the whole process of bringing up the younger generation) help us to solve the terrible problems of society today; but of course this is not the only obstacle. So let us consider what might be the ideal education in terms of man's aims and needs. There is a great variety of natural gifts among human beings, and all these different kinds of gifts are valuable, indeed indispensable, for human welfare. But these human gifts are only potentialities to begin with. They do not become effective realities unless they are stimulated and trained and given opportunities for being used, and this is really what we mean by education in the widest sense.

It is in the interest of both the individual and society that each individual's particular gifts should be helped to bear fruit for the benefit of both the individual and society. We cannot, of course, have a completely different system of education for each individual; yet, as far as possible, the individual's very subtly distinctive personality should be taken into account in giving him his education. I realize that this is difficult. Education has to be standardized to some extent, but it should be as flexible as possible.

At the same time, education has another function. Besides having the function of developing the individual's gifts, education is also the means of passing on our human cultural heritage from one generation to the next. In performing this function too, education ought to be as flexible as possible. In educating members of the rising generation, or rather in helping them to educate themselves, we ought to be trying to help them to equip themselves both morally and intellectually for forming their own judgement on the cultural heritage that is being passed on to them. When the rising generation has reached an age at which it has become mature enough to pass judgement, it ought to be free to retain or to reject or to modify the cultural heritage that is being handed on to it.

I have laid stress on the individual's distinctive gifts and on the need for taking account of these, but, in so far as education is a means of transmitting a cultural heritage, we need to give the same education to all members of the rising generation, whatever may be the differences in their individual abilities. In an ideal education, therefore, there ought to be one side that is individual and is fitted to each particular person, and another side that is common to all members of the rising generation, who will have the common task of taking over the management of human affairs from the generation of their parents.

Now let me come to the present system of education in the formal sense. This is by now the more or less world-wide system of education everywhere in the more advanced countries, and it has been more or less standardized, especially at the upper levels, and at the university level above all. This present modern world-wide system of education is of Western origin, but it has been adopted in countries that have been partly or wholly substituting the modern Western form of civilization and way of life for their own traditional form of culture.

This Western system of education has ancient origins, and it has a very special and peculiar history. You may say that it started in Ancient Greece in the fifth and fourth centuries B.C. In Greece in those centuries, it was invented for educating boys to be citizens of city-states. The same Greek education was continued in Greek and Latin in the Roman Empire for educating boys to be civil servants. Then in the medieval Western Christian world it was modified for educating boys to be Christian priests. But it is now being adapted for educating not only boys but girls—say, Japanese girls, or Indian girls, or Russian girls—for taking up any adult profession or occupation.

This development raises, to my mind, a question. Is it really practical to try to produce a general education for young people of both sexes and of all degrees of intellectual ability out of a special education that has been developed in one particular civilized society for educating the candidates for one particular profession in that society? Is the education which was intended for a thirteenth-century Western Christian priest altogether suitable for a twentieth-century Japanese girl who may be going to become an industrial worker or a secretary or a wife and mother? I also have another question. Is it really practical to impose a single standardized form of education on everybody, considering the variety in the forms of ability, and the differences in degree of ability in any form, between one human being and another?

Some people have a gift for technology, for the mastering of man's non-human environment (I think this gift is by far the commonest among human beings). Some people have the rarer gift for administration, for the management of social relations between human beings, the handling, not of things, but of people and of the relations between people. Other people—this is rarer still—have a gift for art, for adding to nature or improving on nature by art, or a gift for religion, for getting into touch with the ultimate spiritual reality behind the universe. In all these various alternative fields, some of the people who have a particular turn for one kind of ability or the other are merely receptive, some are creative. Some people simply have the ability to take over and hand on what is offered, others can take it over and change it, for better or sometimes for worse. So is a uniform system of education really adequate for catering for all these varieties of human gifts?

And is it fair to the individual, and is it expedient for society, to give the same education, no less and no more, to individuals who have different degrees of ability? This is a burning question in Britain today. Some people feel that so-called comprehensive schools may be going to give a uniform egalitarian education to boys and girls of varying degrees of ability, and that there will not be enough opportunity in such schools for exceptionally able boys and girls to go ahead, as there is in some other schools of an older kind. Anyway, there is much controversy in Britain, and in many other countries too, today, as between egalitarianism and giving the exceptionally able person more opportunity.

I am not entirely neutral in this controversy because I do think that the exceptional ability of a small minority—not just intellectual ability, but ability in each of these different fields of human activity that I have mentioned—is the only capital that the human race possesses. I believe that this is what has made mankind's fortune. When we think in terms of teeth and claws and fur and muscular power and speed, human beings are completely outclassed by other species of living creatures. It is our mental ability alone that has given us the ascendancy over our fellow creatures— our mental ability applied in the first instance to making tools, to technology, and then applied to more spiritual and less material uses of ability. If we were to deprive exceptional individuals of the opportunity to develop and to use their ability by imposing on them a uniform egalitarian education, we should, I feel, be frustrating them unjustly and we should also be depriving society in a very improvident way of the human capital that is society's sole resource for improving the material and spiritual conditions of human life.

Exceptionally able individuals ought to be given, I should say, the best education from which they are capable of profiting. I also think that these able individuals should be required, in return for being given this opportunity by society, to use their exceptional personal gifts for the benefit of society. At the same time, all individuals should be given an education of some kind, because education in the broad sense is necessary in order to enable the human being to become a participant in society. We must all become participants, whatever our degree of ability, because man is a social animal. We cannot change that.

I am now going on to discuss education from the point of view from which we distinguish a special education for an intellectual élite from a mass democratic education. Is it still possible, as it was in the past, for an educator in the higher levels—the university levels—of education to combine doing original research and writing of his own with carrying on at the same time a very exacting teaching job? This is a crucial question at the present time. Is it any longer practicable or expedient that the same person should try to play both the role of the educator and that of the creative intellectual, artistic, and spiritual worker?

In the past, the distinction was drawn between higher and lower education on the basis of the respective roles that the teacher and the learner were expected to play at these two different levels. At the lower level the teacher was expected simply to transmit the existing heritage of knowledge and understanding. He was not expected to add to this heritage himself. But at the higher level the teacher was expected to be a creator as well as a transmitter, and it was held to be of the essence of higher education for the pupil that he or she should be in personal contact with a teacher who was adding to the cultural heritage besides transmitting it. The learner at the higher level of education was to learn how to become a self-educator and, if possible, a creative worker like the professor whose pupil he was.

The traditional combination of the two roles of educator and creative worker at the level of higher education has had more than one historical cause. It was rightly held to be inspiring for the pupil. It was also found convenient economically, because the fees paid by the student for being taught financed the university teacher's own creative work. Creative work does not bring in immediate returns. It may never bring in any practical returns at all (though it often does); so it might have been difficult to finance creative intellectual work if it had not been combined with teaching.

I think that this combination is, and always has been, a difficult one. Some people have a vocation for teaching; others have a vocation for creative intellectual and artistic work. The born teacher is glad to have the cultural heritage as an instrument for use in education. The born creative worker finds it sometimes excruciating to have to use the cultural heritage for this utilitarian purpose. What the creative worker wants to do with the cultural heritage is to work on it, to improve it, and to add to it, not to use it as an instrument for teaching.

Let me draw on my own experience. I myself, at the beginning of my adult career, obtained a teaching post at Oxford in a college at which the students' average standard of intellectual ability was high. But I soon came to feel that my duties as a teacher were interfering with my ambition to be a creative worker. Taking tutorials, giving lectures, correcting examination papers, were consuming more of my time and energy than I was willing to give to this kind of work. More serious still, I felt that the inevitable repetitiveness of a teacher's work was blunting the cutting edge of my mind, and I wanted to keep my mind's edge sharp in order to use it for creative work. For this reason I gave up teaching and I have not returned to it. I have managed to earn my living in other ways that did not blunt my mind, and that left me a margin of leisure for doing creative work which might not earn money. Thus I myself did not find the double role of being a university teacher and a creative intellectual worker congenial.

This is a personal answer to the question, and this was also more than half a century ago. Since then, the demands made by both teaching and research have become more exacting, and most universities now also have to carry an increasing burden of administrative work as the population of a university grows in numbers. Hence there is now a tendency for university staffs to split between eminent scholars who devote themselves to research and to creative work, without having much personal relation with their students, and junior lecturers who do not have much more time for doing creative work, and perhaps do not have much more ability either, than the average teacher in a secondary school. A rich society can now afford to release eminent scholars from teaching and allow them to devote themselves wholly to their own research and creative work. But this may have an unfortunate effect upon teaching at the higher level; and this is, I suppose, one of the many reasons for the present unrest among university students.

The openings for entering a university are much more widespread than in the past, and this is a very good thing; but, just because of this, the educational opportunities at a university, at a large university anyway, are now all too often poorer than they used to be. The students are handed over to junior lecturers and to academic administrators. Personal contact with eminent scholars is no longer open for students, and therefore the students feel that they have been cheated. They are not being given the kind of education that the word 'university' seemed to them to be promising to them. Yet, if the scholars were, as before, at the students' disposal, the scholars might be overwhelmed by the sheer number of students. They might be frustrated and stultified.

Perhaps the remedy is to have different levels of university, and to keep the universities with the highest level down to the traditional size, that is to numbers that are small enough to make personal relations between students and professors still practicable. I think that the entry into these higher-level universities should be by merit—I mean by ability to profit from the opportunity; I am not speaking of merely intellectual merit. And I think that the release of a professor's time from teaching for research and writing should also be by merit. But perhaps every professor should be required to do a minimum of teaching, mainly in the form of discussion groups.

A researcher and writer who, like me, for instance, found even this amount of teaching uncongenial, should be provided for, if his work is valuable enough, in a research institute which does not offer teaching even for post-graduate students. The majority of the students who want to go further than the stage of secondary education should be provided for, I think, in two-year colleges.

Here there would be no pretence that they were going to receive a university education of the highest kind. I should guess that only a rather small percentage of young people above secondary school age can really benefit by a university education of this highest kind. This, however, is just a guess, and I have not offered a solution of the problem created by the tension between the vocation for educating people and the vocation for doing creative intellectual and artistic work of one's own.

We have not yet discussed the special problems in the field of education which arise from the fact that people—industrial workers, in particular—have been given by technological progress (especially automation) more spare time than they can use profitably and to their own satisfaction. This is a modern problem and it is a serious one. In the pre-agricultural age, man had abundant leisure. Leisure was forced on him by nature at seasons when there were no edible berries to be found and when the birds and animals and fish that were his prey were not within his reach. Even after the invention of agriculture, which was the first big step towards keeping people busy and towards regimenting human life, there were close seasons; there were long winters with long nights, especially in high latitudes, in which people could not work. They might become half-starved before the ripening of the next crop of wild berries, or of cultivated cereals or rice, but they did compulsorily have time to think and to do creative artistic work, and time to practise religious contemplation.

In early human society the individual's life was not yet detached from the collective life of the community. Even religious contemplation and intellectual thinking were not done in isolation, and creative work—singing, dancing, ritual, visual art—was intensely corporate. Therefore even individuals who had no special personal gift or inclination for any of these activities were stimulated to use their leisure in positive ways, thanks to their participation in the community's life.

The Industrial Revolution liberated man from, or deprived man of, the leisure time that had been imposed on him by the alternation of the seasons. Machines can work for twenty-four hours a day for 365 days a year. Machine-driven man had to be given compulsory leisure artificially, to save him from being worked to death. But the industrial worker's use of this compulsory leisure has been mostly negative, so far.

Moreover, the mechanized system of industrial production arose, and this not by accident, in Protestant Christian countries in which, contrary to the teachings of the Christian gospels, work was equated with activity and virtue and success, while non-work was equated with idleness and vice and failure. It may be true that, in the past, a majority of the privileged minority who were exempt from having to work in order to earn their living misused their leisure by idling their time away on frivolous occupations, or on simply doing nothing. There is a word in the Turkish language, *keyf*, which means spending your time vacuously with an empty head, doing nothing at all, and this, to the old-fashioned kind of Turk, was the nicest way of spending his time that he could imagine. But a minority of this privileged minority did use its leisure-time for positive purposes, and it is this minority of a minority that has created human culture.

In our time the continuing progress of technology is beginning to create more and more compulsory leisure. But in industrialized man the faculty for using leisure has become atrophied and the traditional collective community life has disintegrated. Modern man often positively dreads leisure, because it confronts him with his own self, isolated terrifyingly in 'the lonely crowd'. He is also still inclined to associate non-work with failure and even with sin. He therefore occupies his off-time either with mock work such as organized games, or with passive spectatorship, watching professional players or viewing television. This is alarming, because it is sub-human. The faculty for using leisure positively in intellectual, artistic, and, above all, religious activities is of the essence of being human.

Modern urban work is not only monotonous; it is also psychologically upsetting because of the boredom that it induces, the overcrowding, both in the work-room and in the street, the noise, the traffic jams, the frustration of our efforts to get about the city. The monotony and the psychic strain are one cause—perhaps the main cause—of the aggressiveness and violence and unrest which we are experiencing all over the World. Then there is a still more alarming point: in the quite near future, the people who can get even this monotonous urban work will be a privileged minority. The population-explosion in the undeveloped countries coincides in the developed countries with the effects of technological progress in making labour superfluous, and not only physical labour; even some brain-work is being taken over by computers. And this technological revolution is spreading to all countries.

In the past, the privileged minority have been rentiers, subsidized to spend their leisure on art, intellectual work, and religion as well as on play. In the age of automation the privileged minority will be the highly skilled technicians who will make, tend, and repair the machines and who will therefore monopolize power.

If we do not take care, the destiny of the great majority of this planet's doubled or trebled population might be to live unemployed in shanty-towns, subsisting on an inadequate dole which would be given to them grudgingly by the productive minority, who would themselves be living in fear of being massacred by the resentful unemployed majority. The productive dominant minority might attempt to forestall any attempt by the majority to depose it by pitting its numbers against the minority's skill and power. The minority might try to protect itself by herding the masses into reservations, fenced in with electrified barbed wire; or they might try to exterminate them, as the natives of Tasmania, Australia, the United States, and Brazil have actually been exterminated to a large extent in the modern age. But in view of the great disparity in numbers between the unwanted, unemployable majority and the productive minority, it seems to me more probable that it would be the minority that would be largely exterminated. If that were to happen, the majority would soon be reduced in numbers drastically by famine and disease and mutual slaughter, and then mankind would find itself back in the state which it left behind at the dawn of the Upper Palaeolithic Age.

This prediction may sound like a fantastic nightmare, yet it may come true if we do not take active steps to prevent it from happening. If we are to avoid this situation, the unemployed majority will have to be given more than a mere dole by the productive minority; they will have to be subsidized generously, tactfully, and in a creative way. We shall have to share out the fruits of technology among the whole of mankind. The notion that the direct and immediate producers of the fruits of technology have a proprietary right to these fruits will have to be forgotten. After all, who is the producer? Man is a social animal, and the immediate producer has been helped to produce by the whole structure of society, beginning with his own education. So it is not reasonable that he should claim to have a proprietary right in his product, and, under the new conditions of automation, this will certainly not make any sense at all. Our future principle will have to be: 'To every man according to his needs rather than to every man according to his production.' And then, when we have met man's material needs, we must give him scope for meeting his spiritual needs. We shall have to overcome the feeling that it is almost disgraceful to be unemployed in the technical sense of not being employed on work for which one is paid a salary. The Buddha and Jesus were unemployed in this sense—that is to say, in economic terms. They would have been labelled in the present world as being unproductive economically and therefore unsatisfactory. But no one would venture to say that they were in fact unproductive. It is only if we were to confine our definition of productivity to material production that we could call the Buddha and Jesus unproductive.

The material side of human nature is not an end in itself. It is only a means to an end. I have already shown that I believe that the true purposes of human life are spiritual; surely we ought to try to make machinery our servant for helping us to carry out these spiritual purposes. It will be our master, perhaps, in the sense that we shall have to live in the uncongenial environment of factories and offices in great cities; but, in any environment, we can lead the spiritual life; and this is what man is for.

Human beings, for the most part, quickly become bored with idleness, and sooner or later, I think, they also become sated with watching sport, and even with taking part in it. The unemployed majority will have to be encouraged to find satisfaction in some non-economic employment. In other words, they will have to be educated in the proper use of leisure. I have already indicated the non-economic fields of activity in which I believe that there is boundless scope for an unlimited number of people. Thought and art and religion are the fields in which the spiritual side of human nature can find infinite scope. It will be difficult, and it will take time, to re-educate industrialized man, or show him how to re-educate himself, so that he can make positive use of his leisure. If we can succeed in doing this, we may see a new flowering of culture—a second Renaissance—instead of the development of a parasitic society, which, like the urban proletariat in the Roman Empire, lives for 'bread and circuses' and turns savage if it is not given them.

One question that remains to be discussed while I am dealing with education is the important question of how far education can help us towards attaining the goal of the unity of mankind. I have no doubt that co-operation in the field of education is one of the indispensable means for knitting the whole human race together into a single family and thus avoiding the danger of mutual extermination in an atomic war.

The period of life at which it is easiest to fraternize is childhood and youth. In those earlier stages of human life, human beings are conscious of their common humanity. They are not alienated from each other by differences of race or nationality or religion. When I walk about the streets of London I see school-children of different races going to and from school, apparently quite unconscious of the difference of race and entirely friendly with each other. It is only as they grow older that some of them come to feel hostility towards each other on account of race.

In the Western world in the Middle Ages, students used to move round from one university to another; they all felt at home in each university. This was easy because, in the Middle Ages, Latin was the common language of Western higher education. Everybody who had had any education could speak some kind of Latin. It might have been a Latin that would have set on edge the teeth of a classical Latin writer, but it was a means of communication, and a very effective one. As a matter of fact, colloquial

Latin went on being spoken in Eastern Europe, in Poland and Hungary, right into the nineteenth century. I once met an old Polish nobleman who could still speak colloquial Latin. I met a Hungarian cardinal who could do the same. I think 1846 was the year in which Latin ceased to be the language spoken in the Hungarian Parliament. Latin was a neutral language which belonged to everybody, but, when it was given up, a question arose: which of the many languages of Hungary should be the parliamentary language? It was a great misfortune for the unity of the Western world that Latin ceased to be a Western international language.

In the German-speaking Western countries where German is a common language, as it is between citizens of Germany and Austria and the German-speaking part of Switzerland, it is still the practice for students to wander round from one university to another. I think this is very educational.

In the Islamic world, students of many different races and languages still meet each other in the Al-Azhar University in Cairo. I have visited Al-Azhar and I found that, as in medieval Western universities, in Al-Azhar they have different houses for most of the nations and most of the languages of the Islamic world, and in Arabic they have a common learned language which is the equivalent of medieval Western Latin.

In Japan, after her conversion to Buddhism, Japanese monks used to make the hazardous sea-voyage to China to visit Buddhist holy places there. I have read in translation the travels of a ninth-century monk, Ennin, who set his heart on visiting a particular Buddhist shrine in the north-east of China, and finally arrived there after many adventures. This was good for international education.

In modern times there have been attempts to create some artificial language such as Esperanto in order to overcome the difficulties in the way of freedom of communication which are created by differences of language.

Artificial languages are handicapped in two ways. They have no literatures and no emotional associations. Their lack of literature is perhaps not a serious handicap for the majority even of literate people, since they do not read much beyond newspapers and magazines. The fatal handicap is the lack of emotional associations. It is these that have made possible the *tour de force* of reviving Hebrew and Irish and Norwegian.

Hebrew had, for centuries past, been used solely as a liturgical language. The *lingua franca* of the Jewish diaspora had come to be Yiddish (a dialect of German written in the Hebrew alphabet). Norwegian had become a peasant patois. Educated Norwegians had taken to speaking and writing Danish with a Norwegian pronunciation. Irish had ceased to be spoken except by a few fishermen on the west coast of Ireland and on the offshore islands; most Irishmen had become English-speaking. The resuscitated Hebrew, Norwegian, and Irish languages are virtually artificial products. Each of them has had to invent a large new vocabulary for conveying modern ideas and for describing modern things. The incentive in each case has been national feeling, and in the Jewish case this has been reinforced by religious feeling, since, for Jews, nationality and religion are inseparable. Thus the incentive for reviving Hebrew has been stronger than the incentive for reviving Norwegian and Irish, and it is no accident that, of the three revivals, the resuscitation of Hebrew has been by far the most successful. In Israel, Hebrew has become a genuine national language, in spite of the existence of Yiddish, which had produced a notable literature and had won a considerable emotional attachment.

Emotional incentives for learning Esperanto are lacking, and I therefore guess that mankind will not adopt an artificial *lingua franca*, convenient though this would be.

As I have said, the younger one is, the easier it is to learn to understand and speak a foreign language and to adapt oneself to foreign manners and customs. But even for the young it is a great aid to intellectual and social intercourse if there is some common international language, such as Latin was in the medieval Western world.

In Eastern Asia, the Chinese characters used to provide this common language in a visual form, though not in an aural or vocal form. Japanese and Korean and Vietnamese monks and literati (scholars) were able to read the Chinese classics and the Chinese translations of the Buddhist scriptures in Chinese characters. While the Roman Empire existed, Greek and Latin provided two international languages for the western end of the Old World and, in the same western part of the world in the Middle Ages, not only Latin but also Old Slavonic and Arabic played the same role as far eastward as the western edge of India.

Today we have to knit together not just local regions, but the whole face of the planet, and there is no world-wide international language ready to hand. In the Western countries since the end of the Middle Ages the use of Latin as a regional common language has been superseded by the cultivation of the local national languages. During the last five hundred years in the Western countries, there has been an almost fanatical insistence on using one's own local national language, and this has spread from the West to other parts of the World. In the West, English and French have had a fairly wide currency, but neither language has succeeded in playing the role which was once played by Latin. During the so-called Colonial period, when a great part of the World was dominated culturally as well as economically and politically by half a dozen West European countries, French and English and Spanish and Dutch did win a very wide currency, but they were in competition with each other. There has been no single world-wide *lingua franca* so far.

The lack of a single world-wide *lingua franca* does create a formidable problem for international education. This will have to start by being polyglot. People who want to have an international education will have to be able not only to read but to write and speak more than one language. Here a very good example has been set for the whole world by the Dutch. In the Colonial age the Dutch language was very widespread. It was the chief—perhaps the only—European language that was known in Japan; it was also the chief European language known in Russia at the time of Peter the Great. Dutch was, I believe, the principal international language of the Svoboda, the Western residents' suburb outside Moscow which Peter used to visit when he was starting to westernize Russia.

The Dutch language has long since lost this international role, but the Dutch have offset this loss by hard intellectual work. They have distinguished themselves by learning to speak English and German and French as well as their mother-tongue. Netherlanders of all social classes and income-levels can generally speak more than one foreign language. I was once having my baggage carried for me at the railway station of Haarlem in Holland, and I asked the porter how many foreign languages he spoke. He said four. I asked him which four, and he said, 'French, German, English, and American.' I thought I had caught him out, and so I said, 'Say some American and say some English.' He said the American with the American accent and the English with the English accent. I said, 'How did you learn that?' He said, 'By carrying their bags as I am carrying your bags now.'

Then once, in Venezuela, I was having dinner with the local head of the Shell Oil Company, which is an Anglo-Dutch company. He was a Netherlander, and he and his wife had sent their children home to school in Holland. I discovered that those children were having to learn (of course) the Dutch language and literature, but also English, French, German, Latin, Greek, and, on top of this, mathematics and all the sciences. Perhaps only the Dutch or the Germans—perhaps the Continental Europeans in general—would submit to such a massive education as that. Yet something like this is the ideal that we have to aim at. Even if we cannot emulate the Dutch, we ought to do our best; and we ought especially to acquire the Dutch freedom from nationalistic language-fanaticism.

However, the mastery of several languages in addition to one's own mother-tongue is merely one of the enabling conditions for becoming an effective citizen of the World. The chief positive qualification for this is that, like the Dutch, we should treasure and love the cultures and the ways of life of the other peoples of the World. We must feel that these other cultures are not 'foreign'; that they are a precious part, like our own local culture, of mankind's common cultural heritage. Here again, love is the key.

Among various proposals for promoting international education, a United Nations University seems to me to be a promising project. It might be wise to locate it far away from the seat of the United Nations' political work and to choose for its location some country that is not a great power politically and yet is cosmopolitan in its traditional outlook.

I come back to the Dutch. I think the Netherlands would be one of the obvious places for a United Nations University, but there are alternatives—for instance, some country in the New World, Canada, for instance, or some non-Western country in the Old World. I suggest Tunisia or the Philippines. The qualifications, besides the negative one of not being a great power, would be geographical accessibility, friendly political relations with the rest of the World, and the currency, in the chosen country, of one or more of the most widespread languages as the local international language, if not as the host country's mother-tongue. In Canada both French and English are native languages. The French-speaking Canadians rather unwillingly learn English, but so far most of the English-speaking Canadians refuse to learn French. Perhaps the establishment of an international university in Canada might stimulate the Canadians to take the obvious step of making the whole of the rising generation of Canadians bilingual. Tunisia, too, is a promising possible location, because here Arabic is the native language and French is the *lingua franca*, and these are two very widespread languages. In the Philippines both Spanish and English are local *lingue franche*.

The international university, wherever located, would have to be polyglot—to do its business in more than one language—but some limit would have to be placed on the number of languages used. This would be a practical necessity, though the choice of the languages would cause severe heart-burnings. I suggest that the international university's official languages, at any rate at the start, should be French, English, Arabic, Spanish, Russian, and Chinese. Speakers of German, Italian, Portuguese, and Persian (Farsi) would, I am afraid, feel aggrieved. They would point out that very large sections of the human race speak their languages and that there are great literatures written in these languages. But you cannot expect many people to be proficient in as many as ten languages.

Some English-speaking people believe that it is the manifest destiny of the English language to become the World's sole international language. Well, two thousand years ago, at the time of Christ, Greek speakers, equally plausibly, had the same expectation about the Greek language, but this did not happen. Greek is not the World's international language today.

It is still more widely assumed today that the Latin alphabet is destined to become the World's universal script, and there have been some events that point in that direction. For instance, in Turkey, since the nineteen-twenties, the Arabic alphabet has been abandoned in favour of the Latin alphabet. Turkish is now written in the Latin alphabet. In Vietnam, the local language used to be written in the Chinese characters, but it is now written in the Latin alphabet, with special signs to mark the differences of tone (like Chinese, Vietnamese is one of the tone languages). This points in the direction of the Latin alphabet prevailing; yet I should not wonder if, by the time that my great-granddaughter, who is now aged four or five, reaches my own present age of eighty-two, a drastically reduced and simplified set of the Chinese characters were to have become the world-wide visual code for international communication, just as the so-called Arabic numerals have become the world-wide code for writing numbers.

This may sound strange at first, because ideograms, such as the Chinese characters, are more complicated than the letters of an alphabet, and they have to be more numerous because they express, not elemental sounds, but ideas. But ideograms have one great advantage: sounds change, whereas ideas are relatively constant. Let me illustrate what I mean. If a fifth-century B.C. Greek could come back to life and go to Greece and try to talk to the present-day inhabitants of Greece, he would not be understood. He and they would both be speaking Greek, but the sounds and the grammar and the vocabulary of Greek have changed so much in the meantime that the Ancient Greek revenant and our modern Greek contemporaries would not be intelligible to each other. But if a fifth-century B.C. Chinese, say Confucius, were to come to life again and were to meet, let us say, Chairman Mao, they would not attempt to talk to each other; they would be aware that, if they talked, they would be as unintelligible to each other as the two Greeks; instead of talking, the two Chinese would write to each other; and the same characters, arranged in the same order, would convey the same meaning to Confucius and to Mao. So there is some advantage in the Chinese characters. This is a point that should be borne in mind by those of us who now use some form of the alphabet. The irresistible tendency for the sounds of any language to change is a drawback to the use of the alphabet in any form, not only in the Latin form but also in the others—the Greek, Russian, Arabic, Hebrew, and so on. Already, the letters of the Latin alphabet are given distinct phonetic values in each of the numerous languages that are written in the Latin alphabet today. This weakness is inherent in the alphabetical system of writing, and it is a serious limitation on the usefulness of the alphabet as a medium of communication between people who speak different languages as well as between the readers of any single language that has undergone changes of pronunciation in the course of time.

6

Society under Pressure from Technology

WAKAIZUMI: Society is becoming vaster and more complex. Can we find ways and means of making it possible for the ordinary individual citizen to participate effectively in the management of affairs? Vastness and complexity tell in favour of management by technical experts and bureaucrats. The unrest of the young and the poor and the penalized is frequently boiling over into violence. How can we make man feel more willing to play a part in this new complex society? Can he retain his liberty without 'dropping out' of the system? Furthermore, how great is the danger that the 'backlash' of insurgency may be dictatorship? Can a unified world state be established in which freedom for all will be a reality? What can be done to avoid the calamity of a tyrannical dictatorship?

Established codes of sexual conduct, like established forms of religion, are losing their hold. Is being human compatible with indulging the physical appetite of sex without the establishment of any abiding spiritual and institutional relation between the parties? Are marriage and the family indispensable institutions? Would children be able to grow up normally and happily if they were deprived of the family setting that, hitherto, they have always had in some form? And what is going to be the role of women? How far will this be affected by the mechanization of life, and how far is a woman's life bound to be governed, under all technological and social conditions, by her built-in physiological constitution and functions?

What are the prospects for the poverty-stricken majority of mankind in a world in which wealth is still unevenly distributed as between rich and poor countries and between the rich and the poor within each country? Poverty seems to be aggravated by urbanization and automation. Then is technology an enemy of progress?

Now that the application of science to technology has so greatly increased mankind's aggregate skill and wealth, what are the right priorities for the use of our resources? This question of human priorities has been raised by the recent huge expenditure of resources on spacemanship while the great majority of the human race is still poverty-stricken.

In the atomic age, has a world government become a necessity; and, if it has, is it attainable? Can political unification on a global scale surmount the obstacles in its path: for instance, differences of culture and of language, nationalism and race-feeling, and the achievement of unification on a scale that is not global but is only regional? Can the United Nations become the embryo of a world government?

TOYNBEE: Man is a social animal. If our ancestors had not already been members of a society, it seems improbable that they would have become human. They had to be social before they could become human, and we, their human descendants, could not survive if society were to dissolve. We are social creatures both by our built-in nature and from economic necessity. Without co-operation we cannot make our living. Society can survive the dropping out of a few individuals, either as hermits or as hippies who may or may not be going to become St. Francises; but even they are still members of society. You may call them parasitic members if you disapprove of them, but they *might* become founders of new societies. I think escapism is a blind alley, and, if the hippies were to end in mere escapism, their protest against present-day society would be useless.

Under the modern conditions which have been created by technology and by the great increase in the number of human beings, the individual's participation in society's life is becoming more difficult. It is hard to see whether we can reform our society and our political systems so as to make participation more easily possible.

I would say that participation in government, the taking of a share in deciding how human affairs are to be managed (and that is what we mean by government), is one of the natural human rights of every individual who is grown-up, who is sane, and who is not a criminal.

Political participation may take many different forms. In a small political community it can be direct, as in a Greek city-state or in a Neolithic village or in some of the smaller present-day Swiss cantons. There are some Swiss cantons, I believe, where every adult male still attends the canton assembly under arms, carrying his gun.

I have seen direct democracy functioning in an Ethiopian village. The night before, a house had been burned down and the question was: had this been an accidental fire, or had it been arson? The village priest had taken the chair; every man, woman, and child in the village had turned up; and they were having a general discussion to discover whether the fire had been accidental or deliberate. This was direct democracy in a rather primitive society. It was possible because the numbers of the population of the village were very small. They could all meet in a single assembly to transact business; but this did need a certain amount of discipline. It depended on their feeling respect for the status and ability and fair-mindedness of the priest who was presiding.

Alternatively, in a larger community, participation can take the representative form, as it does in countries with parliamentary constitutions. Under this régime the individual does not take part directly in the decision of public affairs, but he elects a representative who takes part directly on his behalf. Even in the most democratic possible representational régimes the political choices, which may involve issues of life and death for everyone, are actually made by quite a small number of politicians. Probably there are any number of other participational forms of political constitution that have not yet been tried. Yet I can think only of direct democracy or of representational democracy as having been actual historical forms of democratic political constitution. When I think of the shape of a knife or a kettle or some other material product of technology, I can find dozens of different shapes; but, when I think of the shapes of constitutions, the numbers are very few and the distinctive types are rare even when I do not confine my survey to institutions that are democratic. We are much less inventive and resourceful about human affairs than about technology.

It is always difficult to forecast the future. The state of society since 1914 was unexpected and unforeseen by my parents, and therefore also by me while I was growing up. We had been expecting that the tendency which had been dominant in the Western world since before the close of the seventeenth century would persist there and would also assert itself in the non-Western parts of the World. We had expected that life throughout the World would become more rational, more humane, and more democratic, and that, slowly but surely, political democracy would produce greater social justice. We had also expected that the progress of science and technology would make mankind richer, and that this increasing wealth would gradually spread from a minority to the majority. We had expected that all this would happen peacefully. In fact, we thought that mankind's course was set for an earthly paradise, and that our approach towards this goal was predestined for us by historical necessity. (You will notice that, in believing in the inevitability of progress in the direction which seemed to us to be desirable, we were Marxians without realizing this.)

The increase in material wealth that we were expecting has actually been achieved, and this far more quickly and more abundantly than we had foreseen. There has also been a tendency towards greater social justice in the distribution of wealth, though, on the other hand, a minority in the rich countries, as well as the majority in the poor countries, has been growing relatively poorer. What we did not foresee was the great moral regression in people's treatment of each other. In the year 1700 the Western world was much more humane than it had been in the year 1600. People were no longer cutting off each other's heads or burning each other to death for political or religious reasons. But in 1971 the World is much less humane than it was in 1913. We have to face the possibility that the World will become still more inhumane by the end of the present century.

Technology applied to weapons makes the slaughter in war greater than ever before, and the invention of bombing from the air has abolished the distinction between combatants and civilians that had been established before the close of the seventeenth century. By the year 1700 in the Western world, war had become a contest between professional armies. It was a game between governments, no longer a fight between peoples. When a province was conquered by one government from another, the private lives of the inhabitants of the province were not seriously affected. They had to transfer their political allegiance, but they were not evicted from their homes or despoiled of their property. The partitions of Poland, for instance, were political crimes, but private life in the former territory of the Kingdom of Poland-Lithuania went on

much as before. In 1971, in the World as a whole, we find ourselves back in an age which resembles the age of the Protestant-
Catholic wars of religion in the West in the sixteenth and seventeenth centuries. We are back in an age of intolerance, animosity,
unrest, and violence, both in the domestic life of each local
sovereign state and in the international relations between these
states. This condition of increasing social anarchy appears to me to
be incompatible with the demands of technology, because technology requires an increasing regimentation of life, an increasing
degree of order and regularity. The tension between technology's
requirements and the temper of mankind in our time is becoming
more acute. This is understandable (I have already discussed some
of the reasons for it); but I do not think that this tension can continue for much longer without being resolved, and the alternative
possible ways in which it is likely to be resolved appear to me all
to be drastic.

The practical question is whether any form of participational
government can survive in this age of rapid revolutionary change,
or indeed in any age of rapid change. Participational government,
even of the narrow-based oligarchic type in which only a small
part of the community manages the community's affairs, is slow-
moving and inefficient. Participational government will work only
if there is a margin of safety for delays and for bungling. Dangerous times invite dictatorships. Human beings dislike being governed
dictatorially, but sometimes they resign themselves to this as being
a lesser evil than anarchy.

Let us think of some examples. In China the period called the
Age of the Contending States (Chan Kuo) was terminated by the
dictatorship of the ruler of one state who, in 10 years of intense
warfare, knocked out all the other six surviving states and made
himself sole ruler, the first Emperor of All China, Shih Hwangti.
There was a similar period in Japanese history, and this was brought
to an end by the progressive establishment of a dictatorial government by three men in succession, Nobunaga, Hideyoshi, and
Ieyasu. It took two generations and a half, or three generations,
in Japan. At the western end of the Old World the anarchy produced by the Roman wars of conquest was ended by the dictator-

ship of Julius Caesar and Augustus and by the transformation of the Roman Republic into the Roman Empire, which was a dictatorial régime. It is obvious that the government of the Roman Republic was not democratic. It was a small oligarchy, confined to the Roman nobility. These Roman nobles were extremely able and competent, and so long as they were governing a relatively small state—just a part of Italy or even the whole of Italy—they managed very well. But Rome did not stop at the conquest of Italy; she conquered all the countries round the shores of the Mediterranean Sea, and the Roman nobility, operating an oligarchic republican constitution, proved quite unequal to the task of governing the whole of the Mediterranean world. The republican Roman Government broke down, and it had to be succeeded by a dictatorship. The alternative would have been the dissolution of society.

These examples, which I have drawn from the histories of China and Japan and the Mediterranean world, do raise the question: will our present-day world be able to save itself from self-destruction without having to pay the price of at least a temporary dictatorial régime?

Unfortunately, we all have to agree that a third world war, which would be fought this time with nuclear weapons, is a conceivable possibility. We know that in such a war there would be no victors; all belligerents would be vanquished. If they were not all annihilated, they would all be demoralized in a devastated world. This would be an act of suicidal insanity. War ought to have been abolished the instant after the atomic weapon had been manufactured. It could and should have been demonstrated to the Japanese people by their opponents in 1945 that this invention had made further belligerency impossible for the Japanese and unthinkable for the inventors of the nuclear weapon; and Japan ought to have been offered peace terms that would have been equitable enough and generous enough to make it psychologically possible for Japan to come to terms without feeling humiliated. Instead, we have not only already used the atomic bomb once, but the powers that possess it have embarked on a competition in piling up nuclear armaments which threaten mankind with self-liquidation.

This behaviour illustrates the power of *karma*, the cumulative effect of past acts. The institution of war is now at least 5,000 years old. Our predecessors began to go to war with each other as soon as they had learned to produce a surplus beyond the provision for the bare necessities of life. This cannot have happened until 'Iraq and Egypt had been drained and irrigated and cultivated. They were the first agricultural countries to produce a surplus over and above the requirements for bare subsistence. These 5,000 years are a very short span in mankind's history so far compared to the first million years. Yet the amount of *karma* that the institution of war has accumulated is already formidable.

There is a lyric in Goethe's *Faust*, in the second part of the play, which conveys the essence of the *karma* of war: 'War is the key word. Conquer! It clangs on and on.'

War is a chain reaction. War breeds war that breeds war without end. We ought never to have committed ourselves to this wicked institution, war, and, after we had learned by experience what its nemesis is, we ought to have abolished it at least as long ago as the middle of the third millennium B.C. When I say 'we' I am identifying myself with all people since the beginning of civilization; in particular, for the moment, with the Sumerians, who were the first people to create a civilization and probably the first people to wage wars. By the middle of the third millennium B.C., war had already wrecked the Sumerian civilization. Since then, war has been the death of one civilization after another, but we still go on waging wars, even now that we have invented the atomic weapon.

Can we liberate ourselves from the *karma* of war? If we can, we shall have performed a very great spiritual feat. If we cannot, we are doomed. I believe that the two nuclear super-powers, the United States and the Soviet Union, are trying sincerely to limit their own nuclear armaments and anti-nuclear defences and to persuade all the minor nuclear powers to do the same. Their ultimate aim is to abolish nuclear weapons. I should like to see these weapons abolished and the existing stocks of them destroyed. Unfortunately, the 'know-how' for forging a new stock of nuclear weapons cannot be forgotten, and, if, in a future war that began by being waged only with so-called 'conventional' weapons, one of the belligerents felt itself to be in danger of defeat, and if it possessed the 'know-how' for making nuclear weapons, I fear that it would make them and use them, however solemnly it might have promised to renounce them. Therefore, now that we have entered the atomic age, and that the science of atomic physics cannot be buried in oblivion, I believe that there will be a nuclear world war, sooner or later, unless the institution of war itself is abolished. In the atomic age, we can no longer afford to wage even 'little' wars with relatively innocuous weapons.

The voluntary establishment of a world government with a participational constitution is not impossible, and unquestionably this is a vastly preferable alternative to an atomic world war. But this rational civilized alternative is possible only on one condition. If we are to achieve it, we shall have to be very much more reasonable, self-controlled, patient, forbearing, mutually tolerant, and mutually loving than either we or any of our predecessors have ever been in the past—at any rate in politics. We shall have to rise, in our political dealings with all the rest of the human race, to the standard that some mothers attain in their loving care for their children and in their readiness to sacrifice themselves for their children. This is a very high standard to demand from everyone in the world, not only in family relations, but in politics.

If we are to save ourselves, we shall certainly have to resign ourselves to submitting to a number of political and economic changes that will be highly unpalatable and disagreeable to most people. For instance, the sovereign independence of this planet's 140 local states will have to be subordinated to a world government which will have to be equipped with effective power to stop the local states from going to war with each other any longer. There will also have to be a radical redistribution of the fruits of the human race's productivity as between the rich countries and the poor countries, and, within each of the rich countries, as between the rich majority and the poor minority. Can these necessary reforms be carried out by any régime that is not armed with dictatorial powers? I believe that this is the really big political question that confronts us now.

Of course it would be ideal if we could carry out these reforms voluntarily and in good time, without fighting each other and without hating each other. But we shall have to use whatever means may prove to be necessary, and I therefore have a foreboding that the career of Lenin may prove to be what we call 'the wave of the future'. I think this because the state of the World as a whole in this twentieth century is very much the same as that of Russia during the nineteenth century. The only cure for the decay and collapse of the Tsardom was a more ruthless form of dictatorship. I suppose that many people in Russia do not like the Soviet régime, but they tolerate it because they would like anarchy still less.

Lenin (the one hundredth anniversary of whose birth was in April 1970) had the necessary qualifications for becoming a dictator. He was supremely self-confident; he was utterly ruthless; but he was very honourably and exceptionally distinguished among dictators by being personally disinterested: he was not concerned with his own power or glory or wealth or self-satisfaction. We shall be very lucky if we get a world-Lenin and not a world-Stalin.

In most of the dictatorships that have risen (and fallen) in our time, there have been two components: a party that has seized and held a monopoly of political power, and a leader embodying the party in his personality. The relative importance of these two components has varied. It is impossible to imagine the Italian Fascist Party without Mussolini, or the German National Socialist Party without Hitler. In these two cases, the leader created the party. However, most of the recent dictatorships have been established by some of the officers of the armed forces of the country that has fallen under dictatorial rule, and in some of these cases the head of the dictatorial government has been only a figurehead. The real power has lain with a clique of officers who have not been of the highest military rank, and this 'junta' or 'camarilla' has changed the nominal leader if it has become dissatisfied with him, while the identity of the real gang of leaders has not been disclosed.

The case of the Vichy régime in France during the years 1940–5 shows that, even in a country in which the national consciousness is as strong as it is in France, national interests may be subordinated to class interests by the rich. If the Axis had won the Second World

War and if Hitler's Third German Reich had survived, I think there would have been a conspiracy between the German Nazis on the one hand and the 'Vichysois' and the 'Quislings' in Germany's satellite countries on the other hand to hold down the masses in all the countries under Nazi Germany's domination. I could imagine a conspiracy of this kind on a world-wide scale. I have already suggested that this turns out (on analysis) to have been the political and social structure of the Roman and the Chinese Empire. I can imagine the World being held together and kept at peace in the year 2000 by an atrociously tyrannical dictatorship which would not hesitate to kill or torture anyone who, in its eyes, was a menace to the unquestioning acceptance of its absolute authority. We have previews of the probable character of a future world dictatorship in the present régimes in Brazil, Greece, South Africa, Rhodesia, and the Soviet Union, and in the former Fascist and Nazi régimes in Italy and Germany.

As I look back on the social history of past ages, I do fear that, in the present state of the World, the establishment of a dictatorial world state in the style of the Akkadian, Persian, Roman, and Chinese Empires is the most probable development. The unprecedented advance of technology seems likely to modify the social pattern superficially but not essentially. The pattern seems likely to be modified in two ways. A future world state will be literally world-wide, because modern technology has linked together the whole of the habitable and traversable surface of this planet, together with its air envelope, by a world-wide network of communications. In the second place the world state cannot be established, in the traditional way, by military conquest. Now that governments possess the atomic weapon, a world war could not result in political unification. The only result that it could have would be the physical annihilation of a large portion of mankind. A literally world-wide world state would have to be established by some other means than war.

It is most unlikely, I fear, that it will be established by the will, or even with the acquiescence, of the majority of mankind. It seems to me likely to be imposed on the majority by a ruthless, efficient, and fanatical minority, inspired by some ideology or religion. I guess that mankind will acquiesce in a harsh Leninian kind of dictatorship as a lesser evil than self-extermination or than a continuing anarchy which could end only in self-extermination.

If the reluctant majority does accept this dictatorship on this ground, I think they will be making the right choice, because it would enable the human race to survive.

I can imagine the rise of some new ideology or religion that would be world-wide. I cannot guess what its doctrine would be, except that this doctrine would give priority to law and order over every spiritual value; it would be the doctrine of the riot police, the doctrine of the national guard.

Our scientists may discover how to replace spontaneous evolution by an evolution planned by human wills and applied to human bodies and minds and souls. If this should happen, the future world dictators might attempt to manipulate human genes so as to produce a new variety of human nature, that will be docile, not through voluntary self-discipline, but through built-in heredity. According to Christian doctrine, the angels are like that. Angels are free from sin, not because they are virtuous, but because they are incapable of sinning. They have a built-in incapacity to sin. It might be possible to breed a race of human beings who would be incapable of being anything except what the dictators would want them to be—and that would be something sheeplike, oxlike, docile.

In the last resort, the individual always has been at the mercy of the managers of society, of the 'establishment', under any régime. But the tension between the individual and society was more tolerable so long as the scale of society remained relatively small, and the individual was able to find personal freedom through his participation in his society's communal life. This was a comparatively happy state of affairs. However, the individual is a constant, whereas human society is capable of a virtually unlimited increase in magnitude by means of population-increase, of more elaborate organization, and of mechanization.

Every human being ought to be doing his utmost, all the time, to defend his personal individual freedom of choice against its being taken away from him by fellow human beings who are grasping at power—and power means choosing for other people besides oneself. I fear that the massiveness and the complexity of present-day society, and the vast number of its members, are going to play into the hands of people who are eager to deprive individuals of their power of choice. Most people, except a few saints like St. Francis of Assisi and Pope Celestine V, have a thirst for power when they have a chance of acquiring it. Society is now being progressively depersonalized, but in human relations the great safeguard is personal confrontation. The present mounting tide of unrest and violence all over the World shows itself most conspicuously in situations in which there is a minimum of personal contact. This is obviously true in the case of war. We cannot hate, maltreat, or kill a fellow human being whom we meet face to face as easily and with as good a conscience as we can when we do not know him, or even see him, when we think of him as being the enemy: 'Pandy' or 'the Boche' or 'the Hun' or 'Charlie' ('Charlie' is the American nickname for the Viet Cong and the Northern Vietnamese). And the same effect of depersonalization can, I think, be seen in the daily life of businesses and other large-scale organizations—including large universities—in which the administrators and the mass of people whose affairs they administer as 'labour' or 'manpower' or 'students' hardly ever meet each other and therefore have little chance of coming to understand one another's problems and needs.

However, we have to face the fact that human beings cannot exist in society without accepting a certain amount of discipline, whether it is self-imposed or imposed by others, in the interests both of society and of themselves. To take a modern example, the drivers of mechanically-powered vehicles have to accept discipline imposed on them by the police if they do not discipline themselves, because, without discipline, roads carrying high-powered, fast-moving mechanical vehicles become death-traps. The tending of high-powered machines of any kind, indeed, implies discipline.

By nature, we human beings are wilful and wayward; we are like mules and goats and camels; our impulse is to rebel against attempts to discipline us, to regiment us, to dragoon us. Human beings, therefore, have to be 'conditioned' in order to make them acquiesce in being disciplined. The multitudes who were induced or compelled to drain and irrigate the jungle-swamps of Ancient 'Iraq and Ancient Egypt, which were the seats of the two earliest civilizations, must have been previously conditioned. In their case, I should guess that the conditioner was religion. I think that religion (what I call the 'lower' religion of nationalism) is also the prime conditioner which enables the 'establishment' to turn men into soldiers and train them to kill their fellow human beings without personal animosity but also without compunction.

In the present-day world the principal conditioner is likely to be technology rather than religion, and some of the products of technology are certainly well adapted to prepare human beings for acquiescence in a dictatorial world government.

The individual members of society are now being subjected to an unprecedently heavy pressure of quantities and magnitudes: quantities, above all, of other people, floods of traffic, magnitudes of cities, abundance of things that there are to be known. This vast increase in quantities and magnitudes has put a premium on the organization of people and things by means of machines that are fabulously expensive to construct and that can be operated only by professionals possessing a skill that is beyond the capacity of most people. The examples that spring first to my mind are those of television and computers. These highly elaborate machines need such a vast investment of capital and such complicated and high-powered organization for their operation that the private companies which at present control them are already in some cases almost as powerful as the governments of some of our present local states; and it is not hard to forecast that even the largest and most powerful non-governmental agencies may find operations on this scale beyond their scope and that governments—eventually a world government—may step in to replace them.

I have already said something about television in answering the questions about education, and have made the points that the viewer of a television picture is, so it seems to me, more passive, is less able to distinguish between what is real and true and what is not, and has less freedom of choice, than a reader or a talker. The television viewer is therefore being conditioned to accept whatever the establishment wants him to accept. One of the things that some French people complained of in the de Gaulle régime was that the Government monopolized television, that they could see only what de Gaulle wanted them to see, and that they were deprived of the means of seeing the realities for themselves and deciding for themselves what they wanted to do. It is evident that the television screen would be an invaluable instrument for use in securing the acquiescence of people who disliked the prospect of submitting to a dictatorial world government, and even more valuable for conditioning the masses to accept the kind of régime that such a world government would impose on them.

Computers are now conquering the world by rapid strides because they provide an answer to the problem of how to deal with the quantities and magnitudes which are a feature of present-day society. The computer can deal with vast quantities of information at lightning speed, and it can put this processed information at the disposal of administrators, managers, and governments. Computers can organize human relations on a colossal scale at the price of depersonalizing human beings. They deprive human beings of the possibility of controlling the demands on them by private agencies or public authorities. For instance, taxpayers can no longer check the authorities' demands, which they have to obey, by doing their own calculations. Like television, computers are hostile to the principle of 'do-it-yourself'. Computers can also process a mass of information about an individual's activities and views, and in Great Britain complaints are already being made that this constitutes an unprecedented threat to individual liberties.

I think it is clear that television and computers would be potent instruments for promoting the docility which would be required in a dictatorial world state. I myself, at my present age, do not like either television or computers, because they limit people's freedom of choice; but I realize that this may be to some extent the personal bias of an old man against these new-fangled inventions, and that I may be underestimating their value for society.

If I am right in forecasting that a world dictatorship is likely to be the way in which we shall avoid liquidating ourselves in an atomic war, and if I live to see this development, I should on the whole be optimistic, because I should not expect the dictatorship to be permanent. No human institutions have ever been permanent so far. All régimes have been relatively short-lived since the time when life began to become unstable. This began at the dawn of the Palaeolithic Age, about 30,000 years ago. Since then, the pace of social change has been constantly accelerating. Our scientists tell us that, if we do not liquidate ourselves, our native planet will continue to be habitable by human beings for about another two thousand million years. This would give us time to explore and colonize other planets in other solar systems and perhaps even in other galaxies—planets that might continue to be habitable for a far longer period than two thousand million years. Meanwhile, human nature might possibly be changed for the better by evolution—even, perhaps, by the kind of planned evolution that human beings have already achieved in the case of domestic animals.

Surely our paramount objective now ought to be the negative one of taking care not to liquidate ourselves. If we keep the future open, we cannot be sure that we shall not misuse the opportunities that we shall then be giving ourselves, but at least we shall be allowing ourselves to have a chance of making the reality of human life approach rather closer to our ideals. In envisaging this possibility, I am declaring myself to be an optimist, as I have said.

We now pass from considering the political aspect of man's life as a member of society to the more intimate question of how the world-wide revolution through which we are living affects man's sexual life.

Ever since our ancestors became conscious, sexuality has been one of the awkward features of human nature. Man is one of the sexual animals. Mankind too propagates itself by sexual intercourse and by the procreation of offspring, followed by the death of each generation in turn. There are some kinds of creatures that we choose to call 'inferior', such as the amoeba, which do not propagate themselves in the same way as sexual animals. The amoeba does not have sexual relations and does not suffer death. It propagates itself by fission into pieces, and these divide in their turn. From our point of view, amoebas are a simple and low form of life; yet, if they could have consciousness and could be aware of us, they might think that we were the inferior form of life. In sexual species, nature has to ensure that there shall be effective sexual intercourse by implanting mutual attraction—lust, if you like to call it this—between the sexes. This is no problem for non-human sexual species, because their sexual life, like the rest of their life, is instinctive. But man is not merely a sexual animal; he is also a spiritual being. If he ceases to function as an animal organism, he ceases to be alive, and, like other animals, he gets satisfaction out of the calls of nature: eating, drinking, mating, and so on. But man also feels that behaving as an animal is beneath his human dignity. He both enjoys the satisfaction of his animality and is ashamed of it, and this is very awkward.

Moreover, man can misuse his animality by perverting it. He can eat and drink to excess. Animals generally eat no more than they need for the satisfaction of their hunger. Man can intoxicate himself; he can drug himself. Above all, he can misuse the indulgence of his sexual appetite by, for instance, promiscuity in sexual relations between the two sexes and by having homosexual relations.

Ever since the earliest stage of human history of which we have any surviving records, man has felt the need to humanize his sexual life. He has done this in two ways. First of all, man has made social rules governing sexual relations between men and women. I am speaking here of the institution of marriage. This is an external, formal, legal way of keeping sex in order. In the past, man has also generally discountenanced the indulgence in sexual relations solely for the satisfaction of the sexual appetite without the accompaniment of a permanent relation of love and of mutually felt moral responsibility. To my mind, mutual love, mutual responsibility, mutual consideration are more important than the legal, institutional side of marriage.

Besides, man is a species in which the young take a long time to become capable of looking after themselves without being looked after by their parents both physically and spiritually. Compare the speed at which, in other species of mammals, the young become independent and become able literally to stand on their own feet, to find food for themselves, and to protect themselves. They can do this in perhaps a few months or, at most, a few years. The more civilized human beings become, the longer the period of growing-up and education. Even in primitive societies, children are inducted into life, not by built-in instincts, but by education in the sense of the transmission of a social and cultural heritage to them by their parents and by other members of the older generation.

For these reasons in combination, the family has been an important institution in all human societies so far, though the form of the family has varied very much. There are societies which practise polygamy, one husband having several wives. Others (these are less frequent) practise polyandry, one wife having several husbands. Others practise monogamy; a single man and a single woman are husband and wife. But, in all societies with all these varieties of forms of marriage, there have been definite rules governing family life. These rules have regulated the sexual relations of the parents, and they have provided a stable and secure framework for the education of the children. What children need above all is a sense of security, something definite and fixed, on which they can count; and all forms of marriage-relations, even those which seem to monogamists to be strange and even inferior, do give this sense of solidity and security.

Of course, in all societies at all times, there have been people who have broken the rules, either openly or secretly; but, in spite of these breaches, the institution of marriage has been upheld by custom, by public opinion, and by law, and the observance of the rules of marriage has been normal. If marriage were just disregarded by everybody, of course the institution would break down. So, even where sexual morality has been lax, the breaches have, on the whole, been exceptional. Or, if they have been extreme, then probably the laws of marriage and the rules of sexual relations have been changed. As I have said in discussing religion, I think that any institution, so far from being dependent on remaining rigid and unchanged, only falls into discredit and eventually may cease to function if we cling to forms of it that do not answer to the needs of our present way of life. We ought continuously to be adjusting the outward forms of an institution to harmonize these with the actual changes in our way of life, and I think this is true of marriage as well as of religion.

At the present day in the West, the rate of divorce seems certainly to be increasing, and that seems to be evidence that the traditional Western conventions regarding marriage need to be reconsidered. There always have been conventions in marriage, but there has been a wide variety in, for example, the facilities for divorce for husbands or for wives or for both. Divorce reform in Christian countries means making divorce more easy. In Muslim countries, for instance in present-day Turkey, divorce reform has meant making divorce more difficult. Under Islamic religious law, divorce is very easy, perhaps too easy, so divorce reform means opposite things according to the particular traditional rules governing the institution of marriage in a particular society.

Then there is the question of the licence that may or may not be permissible for non-committal sexual relations before marriage, not necessarily relations with the other person who is going to be one's eventual permanent marriage partner. In many societies, especially in some primitive societies, there has been considerable laxness, and considerable permissiveness of public opinion, towards looseness of sexual relations before marriage. Certainly it used to be so in English villages, and I think it is so still, and there are other societies in which this has been true. It is certainly true of young people in urban communities today all over the World. Evidently this question of sexual relations before marriage needs to be reconsidered. Should they be frowned upon and discouraged? Should they be countenanced within reason? Should they be regulated? Should they be entirely free and promiscuous? If you have extreme sexual licence before marriage, is it possible to settle down to sexual regularity when once you are married? I do think that liberties that traditionally have been banned might need to be reconsidered on their merits in societies in which the present immense technological revolution is changing the external conditions of life, and in which these changes are therefore calling in question the traditional conventions of social behaviour. Technology is concerned primarily with objects, but it does also affect human feelings and actions—for instance, technological inventions like the oral contraceptive, which has introduced a new liberty for indulging in sexual relations without fear of the consequences for the female partner.

Nevertheless, I expect, and I also hope, that the institution of marriage will survive in one or other of the various forms that it has taken in the past, and still takes, in different societies and among the adherents of different religions. I think this because of man's double nature. I do not believe that most men and women will find it permanently satisfactory to confine themselves to a series of temporary, unstable, sexual relationships that do not call forth the spiritual qualities which, as I have said, marriage in any form does call forth. I think that the essence of marriage, under any rules, is bound to be the same; it has to be a stable relationship, maintained, not just by law, but by love, and by love I mean a spiritual partnership, not mere sexual desire. I also think that mankind's spiritual qualities are more often displayed, not only between the husband and the wife, but also in the task of bringing up a family, in a monogamous marriage than in any other form of the institution. I am prejudiced, I suppose, because I have grown up in a society in which monogamy has been the rule. Though in many ways I am a rebel against the society in which I have been born, I find that I do agree with this society's traditional rules about this important particular point.

Childless marriages, too, can be very happy and socially useful. But the common enterprise of bringing up children, the common experience of carrying out this very difficult job, does reinforce the spiritual bond between husband and wife. In cases in which relations between husband and wife have been strained, the marriage has often still been held together by a common concern for bringing up the children.

Even when there are children, monogamous marriage for life is difficult. It is difficult because the males of a sexual species are promiscuous, not monogamous, by nature. Another reason why it is difficult is because human nature is so complex, so subtle, and so various that a perfect match between a man and a woman is bound to be rare. Most marriages require some amount of mutual forbearance, and only mutual love makes this forbearance possible.

Therefore, though I believe that life-long monogamous marriage is the ideal institution, and that it is best for society that this should be the standard normal practice, I also believe that the dissolution of a marriage may be the lesser evil, not only for one or both of the parties, but for the children too, if there are children. I therefore think that public opinion and custom and law ought to be merciful and charitable and flexible in deciding whether or not a marriage should be dissolved. Each case is unique and should be decided on its own merits. The decision is always very difficult both for the parties to the marriage themselves and for the representatives of the law and of public opinion.

It is important to remember that, although marriage is such an intimate affair between a husband and wife, or a husband and wives in the case of polygamous societies, the maintenance or dissolution of a marriage is not exclusively the business of the husband and the wife. Everyone recognizes, of course, that the children's welfare is intimately concerned; but so also is the welfare of society, because the institution of marriage is, in my belief, one of the keys to the maintenance of human society, whatever the particular form of the human society may be.

It is true that the practice of celibacy does also enable the men and women who follow this way of life to rise to high spiritual levels and to perform very useful social functions. But only a very small minority of human beings feel the call to this form of 'dropping out' of normal society, and those that do feel called cannot always stay the course. I have touched on this point in another place.

The modern technological revolution has also affected the nature of the home and people's attitude towards it. Up till now the home—family, husband and wife, children—has been the focal point of man's existence. But now there seems to be a competition between the home and the office, or the home and the factory. The question whether the home should remain the centre of life is now being asked, and the traditional affirmative answer is being called in question. The fact that the garage is such an important part of a recently-built house, and that the car which is housed in the garage is a device for getting away from the home, may be a symptom that the home is, so to speak, loosening up.

Here again I am perhaps old-fashioned. I believe that a home is a psychological necessity for children. The essence of a home is that it is a permanent community of parents and children. The home need not be physically stationary, so long as it makes it possible for the family to keep together. Gipsies have homes on wheels. The nomadic peoples of Asia and Africa are dying out, but many of them, as long as they existed, had homes on wheels, and these were true homes, which held together families that included animals as well as human beings.

In non-nomadic societies—in settled, sedentary societies—till quite recently, most people's homes were identical with their work-places, whether the workers were farmers, or handicraftsmen and women, or were the followers of liberal professions, lawyers and doctors and teachers. Even priests, though they carried out their functions in places for public worship and not in a private workshop or consulting room or office, usually had their home next door to the place where they did their business—next to the temple or church or synagogue or mosque.

Today the home has become separate physically from the factory or office because of the increase both in the physical size of human settlements and in the elaborateness and technicality of the World's work. Most of the World's work today could not be done in the home, as it used to be. It requires very elaborate, dangerous, and in some cases massive machinery. So 'commuting' twice a day between the dormitory and the place where the bread-winner earns his living is a new feature of social life, and this certainly is undermining the home. I have spent quite a time standing at an hotel window in the city of Tokyo, the biggest city in the World, looking down on an eight-track railway and watching the trains bringing in or carrying out commuters, train after train, each about a quarter of a mile long, following each other at a minute or two's interval. I was told that 12,000,000 people sleep in Tokyo, but that 17,000,000 spend the daytime there, so 5,000,000 people go in and out of Tokyo every day.

When the home and the work-place were still not separated, even the children could at least understand the nature of the work by which the family earned its living; and in an agricultural family the children would have a spontaneous, informal apprenticeship. In England I spend part of the year in a rural district, next door to several farms. I know the farmers and their children well, and I know some children who, from the age of about three, trot after their father or their grandfather and help to drive the cows in to be milked, or help their mother or their grandmother to collect the hens' eggs, and so on. They know what the work is about, and they can and do take a useful part in it from a very early age. This is the ideal way of being educated; but today the bread-winner's work is generally invisible and incomprehensible for the rest of the family, for his wife as well as for his children, while for the bread-winner himself the home has become a mere dormitory. He sleeps there and spends the week-ends there, but his effective life is in his work-place, which may be many miles away and which his family seldom visits. They would interrupt his work if they visited his work-place, whereas on the farm they join in his work and help his work by taking part in it.

This degeneration of the home threatens to prize family solidarity apart, to deprive children of the sense of security that they need, and also to deprive them of the natural channel of apprenticeship for adult, responsible, socially productive life. So, although we may have to accept the change in the nature of the home and of its relation to the work-place, the home is surely still indispensable, and it would be a calamity if it were to collapse.

Another question that arises when we think of the effect of the modern revolution on mankind's social life is that of the status of women. We have to face the fact (a shameful one, I think) that, throughout human history and still at the present time, the social status of women has been bad compared to the status of men. Can society reform itself to make the relation between the sexes equal? Can the sexes perform equal social roles and carry equal burdens?

I do not know at what stage of human history people made the scientific discovery that conception and childbirth are consequences of sexual relations. I do not think that non-human animals have ever realized the connection, and I do not suppose that human beings realized it at first, not even after they had awoken to consciousness, though in retrospect it seems a very simple and obvious discovery. The point that I want to make is that this discovery of the fact of paternity was bad for the status of women, because, until it was made, the mother was believed to be the sole parent, and the prestige of women, as the self-sufficient propagators of the human race, must have been very high.

The worship of fertility in the paradoxical form of a virgin female goddess still survives, even in the major branches of the Christian Church. The Eastern Church venerates her as the Theotókos, 'the Mother of God'; the Catholic branch of the Western Church venerates her as 'Our Lady'—a counterpart of her son's title 'Our Lord'. She is really the ancient Neolithic goddess of fertility, the virgin goddess who was also a mother, surviving into the present day and receiving enormous reverence and devotion from generation to generation. The Northern school of Buddhism, too, has recaptured her by changing the sex of one of the bodhisattvas, Avalokita, and transforming him into Kwan Yin (in Chinese), alias Kannon (in Japanese).

In the early Neolithic Age, which was characterized much more significantly by the invention of agriculture than by the invention of a new way of making stone tools, I think the prestige of women must have increased if it is true, as some archaeologists believe, that agriculture was invented by women and was practised by them alone at first. The highest peak up till now in the prestige of women since they ceased to be thought of as the sole parents may have been at the transition from the Palaeolithic to the Neolithic Age, when the women were already raising crops and were thus providing a much more stable food-supply than the game which the men, who were still only hunters, were able to provide.

I think the position of women must have been depressed when society began to produce a sufficient economic surplus to make warfare possible. Until our time, warfare has been considered, in almost all societies, to be exclusively men's work. The Greeks had a legendary people called the Amazons who were female warriors, but no one ever met an Amazon; they were mythical creatures. Socially, I think, it has not been beneficial for women to be exempted from military service, though materially, of course, this has been to their advantage. It has exempted them from wounds and death and danger, but socially it has kept them in an inferior position, because the soldier has had prestige. However, today women are being conscripted, in Israel, for instance, for active military service, besides being exposed to indiscriminate bombing even if they are civilians.

Physiologically, men appear to have a shorter expectation of life than women. If men are not killed prematurely in war, but are allowed to live until they die a natural death, they die younger on the average. But a man is stronger physically than a woman, and this formerly gave men an advantage over women. For instance, a woman could handle a hoe in agriculture; she could hoe a field; but she could not handle a team of oxen yoked to a plough. So when, with the advance of agriculture, hoe-cultivation was replaced by the more efficient technique of ploughing, agriculture passed out of women's hands into men's.

For about 5,000 years, ploughing and war were the two key-occupations in human life, and both were men's occupations. Now, however, there has been a change. The progressive replacement of human and animal muscle-power by the harnessing of the energies of inanimate nature has liberated women from the previous handicap of their relative physical weakness. In tending machines and in doing office-work, women can compete with men on equal terms—in fact, sometimes on more than equal terms, because I think that women have greater patience than men, and they are more willing to take trouble about details, however dull these may be. I think this makes women psychologically fitter than men to endure the monotony of present-day urban industrial work and office-work.

There have been women who have excelled in creative genius as highly as any eminent man. I am thinking, for instance, of a whole series of nineteenth-century English women novelists, who were certainly the equals of the also famous male English novelists of their time. I can think of many other cases; Greek women poets are a notable example. But there have been far fewer women than men who have actually succeeded in coming to the top in any walk of life, in politics or religion or whatever it may be, and this raises a question. Is this because creative genius is in truth rarer among women than among men? Or is it because, since the invention of ploughing and of war, society has been organized for the convenience and for the advantage of men, and women have been under the handicap of having to make their way, when once they get out of the narrow field of conceiving and bearing and bringing up children, in a world that has been organized as a man's world?

This man's world is a social structure, and all social structures can be changed. What I have called the man's world is in fact being changed in our time by the development of machinery and office-work. The typewriter, for instance, is in general a woman's rather than a man's machine. Will the penalization of women be re-dressed by mechanization? Or is there a deeper cause of it? Is the rarity of women who have come to the top so far due to something permanent? Is it due to the difference in the reproductive functions of the two sexes? To bear children and to bring children up takes up more psychic energy, as well as more physical energy and more time, than to be a father. To be a mother and to feel un-fulfilled unless one has become a mother—that is the greatest social handicap of all for women, even in a world in which physical work has been mechanized, and in which women have gained economic and political equality with men. Buddhist and Christian nuns renounce motherhood, but do they make this sacrifice with impunity? Suppose that we took to producing human beings in test-tubes, and thus separated sexual relations from procreation. Would women suffer psychologically from not having children to bear and to bring up? Would men suffer too? Would children of both sexes suffer? We come back to the question whether the institution of the family is indispensable.

There is another query that arises out of this very big question. Can a woman have enough physical and mental energy to pursue a professional career up to the male standard of professionalism, side by side with being a mother? Will not her children suffer, even if she does all that the best mother can do for them? Will her children not be jealous of their mother's professional work? Will they not demand to have the first call on their mother? Is it bad for children not to have the first call on their mother? Or is this perhaps a wholesome and useful part of their education? May it not be a means of teaching them, at an early stage in their lives, that in truth the universe does not centre on them?

I can answer this question *ad feminam* because I have a daughter-in-law who is the mother of six children and who is also a doctor, a general practitioner, part-time. She certainly has not starved her children of love and they certainly do not feel deprived, and she is also certainly a good doctor; her patients, as well as her husband and her children, appreciate what she does for them. She seems, by a *tour de force*, to manage to be a mother, a cook, a housekeeper, and a doctor, all in one. I do not know how common this is, or how possible it is for many people to do it, but I do at least know this one actual case.

I have just referred to the possibility that human beings might be bred in test-tubes, and earlier I have mentioned the part that might be played by selective breeding in conditioning human beings to acquiesce in the establishment of, and the exercise of power by, a dictatorial world government. Till now, human nature has remained a fixed quantity ever since our ancestors became human in the act of becoming conscious. Of course, the change from being pre-human to becoming human was a stupendous natural revolution. It was the greatest revolution, that we know of, in the history of our planet, except for the origin of life itself. Since the date when we became human, we have transformed the natural environment of human life, partly by modifying inanimate objects to suit our human purposes, and partly by domesticating some of our non-human fellow living creatures and breeding them deliberately with a view to making them more useful to us. By selective breeding we have changed some species of plants and animals almost out of recognition. The original wild plant from which our domesticated maize has been bred has not yet been traced. There are still some wild ducks, geese, sheep, and goats, but the domesticated breeds have been differentiated from them, as a result of planned breeding, far more widely than they would ever have been differentiated by natural unplanned evolution during an equal period of time.

Our dramatic success in transforming our domesticated animals by selective breeding is evidence that we could produce comparable changes in human nature by the application to ourselves of the same breeding techniques. We have been inhibited from doing this, partly by ignorance and partly by pride. Till very recently, we have been ignorant of the structure—and indeed of the existence—of genes, and therefore we have not had the power to manipulate them. Now that we are beginning to know how to manipulate genes, our sense of our own human dignity has, so far, restrained us from breeding new varieties of human beings, as if we ourselves were domesticated animals. We cannot yet foresee whether we shall overcome this inhibition or not.

In breeding domesticated plants and animals, man has been interfering with nature for a long time. We have, for instance, killed or castrated all male domesticated animals except a few that we have selected for breeding purposes. We have robbed female cows, sheep, and goats of their milk, and hens of their eggs. We have now started the artificial insemination of cows, and I daresay we shall soon be producing domesticated animals in test tubes.

By selective breeding to develop particular features of a domesticated species of animal, we have proved our ability to change the nature of the species in the ways at which we have been aiming. We have also been able to do this at a speed that is very much faster than the pace of natural selection. It is during the last 10,000 years that we human beings have domesticated all our domestic animals except the dog, and it was not until we had domesticated non-human animals that we began to practise selective breeding and to import human selection into natural selection. Are we now going to breed human beings in the way in which we have already bred domesticated animals and plants so successfully?

If we think of doing this with human society, we shall be faced with two problems: first, what particular features in human nature are we going to choose to develop? Second, what is going to be the psychological effect on human beings of being bred artificially? In the case of domesticated plants and animals, we know what effects we want to produce. Our aim is utilitarian; we want to make these plants and animals serve human purposes more

tury, reckoning down to the date of my birth in 1889, by
king the Industrial Revolution. It is true that this revolution,
most others, had cost a high price in suffering, and that the
eficiaries had been only a minority of the population. For a
siderable section of the still poor majority, the economic
tion and conditions of life had worsened, not only relatively,
also absolutely.

owever, since 1914, the previous gap between rich and poor in
ain has proved not to have been decreed by an inexorable
of nature'. It has not been closed, but it has been greatly
inished by the effects of two things: social welfare legislation
the growth of unionized labour's bargaining power. The rich
been more heavily taxed, and the income of the poor has
raised to higher levels both by the introduction of social
ces, paid for largely out of taxation, and by increases in real
es.

herefore believe that the gap between the rich and the poor
tries could be reduced by similar means. So far, the dole given
he rich to the poor countries in the form of so-called 'foreign
'charity' in the nineteenth-century British domestic termin-
y—has been largely offset by the imposition of unfavourable,
d inequitable, terms of trade on the poor countries and by the
oning off of the profits from industries established in the
r countries by the enterprise, and with the capital, of entre-
urs from the richer countries.

e analogy with what has actually happened in the domestic
f Britain since 1914 suggests to me that the present gap
een the rich and the poor countries could be reduced by two
es in the organization of world affairs. We need a world
nment that will be strong enough to tax the rich countries
y for the benefit of the poor countries. We also need a
ization of the poor countries. The pressure that trades unions
ing on the community by means of strikes is not, I think, a
thing in itself; strikes are a form of militancy, a form of the
ar; but they are a lesser evil than permanent social injustice.
poor majority of the World's countries were to strike
ively, by refusing to sell to the rich countries their labour,

effectively than before. But do we know how, if at all, we wish to
modify our own human nature?

Now that our progress in technology has armed us with annihil-
ating weapons, it is conceivable that we may come to the conclusion that we cannot any longer afford to let nature take its
course in the production of human beings; that we cannot afford
to have anti-social behaviour in an age in which we have equipped
ourselves with atomic weapons. We might decide that we must
sterilize all human males and females before the age of puberty,
and must breed children exclusively from test-tubes out of selected
genes, from which we shall have eliminated those genes that
generate self-centredness, aggressiveness, pugnacity, and anti-
social behaviour of all kinds.

We do not know yet whether we could eliminate undesirable
qualities without also eliminating other qualities that we should
wish to preserve. We certainly do not yet know whether we can
eliminate aggressiveness without also eliminating such qualities as
creativeness, inventiveness, curiosity, adventurousness, energy.
Take the difference between a bull and an ox, which is a castrated
bull. A bull is a dangerous, formidable creature, good for breeding
but not for much else. An ox is very useful, because he is un-
pugnacious and submissive. You can harness him, yoke him, put
him to work. We might find that we had bred a race of docile,
hard-working human oxen. Do we want to do that? And there is
another point. Oxen have un-oxified human beings to breed them
and to set them to work. What would happen to a human breed
that consisted exclusively of oxified human beings? We do not
know the answer to this question, and we are also utterly ignorant
of what the effect on human nature would be of being bred in a
test-tube. Could human beings do without having human mothers?
Probably we shall be compelled by the dangerousness of the
products of our technology to explore these unknown genetic
possibilities, and I think the prospect is alarming. We shall be
groping in the dark, and the results might be irrevocable.

All the same, it does seem not only illogical but also unenter-
prising and cowardly for man to leave the propagation of his own
species at the mercy of nature, when he has successfully imposed

human purposes on nature in either transforming or exterminating so many other species of living creatures apart from his own species.

So far, the problems that we have been discussing have been for the most part those that arise in or between the industrially advanced countries, in which the changes produced by technological progress have had the most effect. But there are also problems arising out of the relations between the advanced, developed countries and the countries which are still industrially undeveloped or under-developed—countries in which technological progress is only beginning to change the conditions of life for most of the population. These are the countries which are the habitat of the majority of mankind, and we have to ask ourselves how we are to make better provision for this still indigent majority. Today, the tension between the fairly rich and the fairly poor countries is growing more acute. Can we close, or at least diminish, the gap between the 'haves' and the 'have-nots'?

Apparently the wealth of a community increases almost automatically when the community has attained a certain level of technological skill, economic organization, and accumulation of capital. On the other hand, if a community fails to raise itself above that level, its material standard of living declines, and this not only relatively to the increasing enrichment of the rich countries; it declines absolutely, because of the population-explosion, which is taking place mostly in the economically and technologically backward countries.

Is this gap inevitable? And is it bound to become wider? The population-explosion has been caused by the technologically advanced countries, I suppose, in the indirect sense that they invented preventive medicine and public health services, and these inventions have now been applied more or less efficiently all over the World, whereas everywhere, even in the advanced countries to some extent, the introduction of family planning has lagged behind the reduction in the rate of premature deaths.

Only the economically backward peoples themselves can take the initiative in resorting to family planning to an extent that will offset the already achieved reduction in their death-rate and so will

re-stabilize their populations—though at a ne has shown that this can be done. Of course, advanced countries, not only in technology b the Japanese example does show that it is wit backward countries too, by their own ac eliminate this cause of their impoverishment.

There is, however, another cause for the ga and the 'have-nots', and this is the manipula trade between the rich countries and the p should guess that Japan is one of the sinners countries in Europe and in North America. in the rich countries' hands, because they stronger of the two parties to trade. I believe reduced, and perhaps could even ultimately countries' present economic policy towar were to be changed to a more equitable and

I am led to this belief by my experience the revolutionary change in the distributio the rich minority and the poor majority Britain. Even the richest countries—even have at least a poor minority in their popula

When I was a child in Britain, human people used to wring their hands over the conditions of life for the poor and for th social worker, who spent his working life help to improve the conditions of the poor he believed sincerely that he was fighting win against an inexorable law of nature. sidize the poor, he believed, the poor wou and would be made incapable of taking tunity for bettering their condition whi them. So, on this view, it would be, if n the poor for the rich to redistribute thei but unachievable benefit of the poor.

In retrospect, I can see that this line of it was, ignored some pertinent historical had raised itself to wealth within a pe

their raw materials, and their foodstuffs, except on more equitable terms, I believe that they could compel the richer countries to change the terms of trade to the poorer countries' advantage; and this would be a victory for justice.

As a result of the redistribution of income in Britain, an increasing proportion of the taxes which finance the welfare state is now being paid by the former poor majority, because their incomes have risen to levels at which tax is payable. I believe that the same result would be produced by an increased subsidization of the poorer countries by the richer countries, accompanied by a change in the terms of trade. If an effective world government were to be established, this could, should, and surely would prohibit all local states from possessing armaments. The vast sums now being spent uneconomically on armaments could then be spent, instead, on improving conditions for the whole human race. If armaments were abolished, the rich countries' subsidies to the poor countries could probably be increased greatly without any proportionate increase in the rich countries' rate of taxation.

For these reasons, I do not think that there is any inexorable natural obstacle to the narrowing of the gap between rich countries and poor countries. I believe that the present widening of the gap is due to deliberate human action (terms of trade) and inaction (failure to practise family planning). This could be changed, and the gap could be narrowed, by deliberate human action. The initiative lies with the rich countries. If they are wise enough to take a long view, they will do what is required, on their part, for closing the gap voluntarily. If they refuse to do this, they will eventually be confronted with a choice between two formidable alternatives. Either they will be deposed by a concerted revolt of the exasperated majority or they will have to hold this majority down by establishing a fascist régime on a world-wide scale.

It is true that the administrators of 'foreign aid' have sometimes found their work on behalf of the recipient nations disheartening. They have been frustrated by the self-seeking, the corruption, and the callousness of the governing minorities that, in these countries, concentrate political and economic power in a few hands. They have also been frustrated by the ignorance, helplessness, and apathy of the poverty-stricken masses. The aid is intended for the masses, yet much of it fails to reach them. It is pocketed, *en route*, by the governing minorities.

This is not an easy problem to solve. The day of colonial rule is over. Even colonial rule by a United Nations civil service, acting as trustees, is no longer feasible. Yet something of this kind is what is needed. In the ex-subject countries, the masses have been 'liberated' from their former foreign rulers, only to be exploited by a powerful minority of their own fellow countrymen. Under these adverse conditions, the so-called 'developing' countries are not being developed. At best they are stagnating; at worst they are regressing. The only remedy for this state of affairs is education, including political education, but this takes time.

As I have just said, I think that a great deal more could be done towards narrowing the gap between the 'have' and the 'have-not' countries if expenditure on help for the indigent majority of mankind were to be given priority over expenditure on armaments. The question of what ought to be the right order of priorities in the richer countries' programmes for distributing their wealth has recently been raised in a specially acute form.

At this point we make a jump, a literal jump, right off the Earth to the Apollo project and to the controversy that the exploration of outer space has raised. Some people are fascinated by it and think that this is a great enterprise which ought to have priority over everything else. Other people deplore it. They feel that this is a waste of our resources and energies and that we ought to get down to other things first. I think this is really a question, not of whether the space programme is good or bad in itself, but of what ought to be its position in our order of priorities. Decisions about priorities are always ethical decisions: what should rightly come first and come last from the point of view of what is just and good for mankind?

I think no one would dispute that, if more pressing demands on mankind's resources and abilities had already been met, the attempt which we are making to break out beyond the bounds of our native planet is an enterprise that is intrinsically noble and is even practically worth while. Adventurousness, directed by intelligence, is one of the distinctive characteristics of human nature, and this is a characteristic in which we human beings may fairly take pride. We admire our ancestors who ventured to fight sabretoothed tigers and to hunt mammoths, to navigate the seas for the first time out of sight of land, and to discover the Americas. Of course, this last mentioned feat looks different from different standpoints. The people who colonized the Americas admire the discoverers, but the discovery of the Americas by Europeans was a calamity for the previous human inhabitants of the region, who were largely exterminated, and for the African slaves who were taken there by force to work for the European colonists. The Chinese and Japanese only avoided the same calamity by being strong enough, in the seventeenth century, to expel the Europeans who had intruded upon Eastern Asia. Still, crossing the Atlantic was a feat of the kind that we admire. So was conveying an army, including elephants, across the Alps, as Hannibal did, or climbing to the summits of the Matterhorn and Mount Everest, or inventing aircraft. Think of the extraordinary bravery of the people who did that. They had crashes again and again in which they broke their limbs or lost their lives, but, at that cost, they invented craft that could, in the end, actually fly. Or think of the people who first tamed horses, which was also a formidable and dangerous feat. We also admire other people who did non-utilitarian things that were not dangerous—the people who built the Pyramids or the Taj Mahal, for instance. We honour the human beings who devoted their lives to great architectural enterprises or who sacrificed their lives in attempting dangerous feats, and we honour equally those people who carried these adventures to successful conclusions. The exploration of space is another enterprise in this series which we can rightly call a glorious series.

Some of these achievements have justified themselves ethically by raising the material and spiritual standard of living for at least a portion of the human race. However, until now, the majority of the human race has been inadequately fed and clothed and housed. This has been a scandal ever since the privileged minority first began to have at its command a surplus which it was free to spend on superfluities and luxuries. Louis XIV's palace at Versailles offends against my sense of social justice. When I visit Versailles I find myself wishing that the French Revolution had followed quickly enough for Louis XIV to have been guillotined instead of his inoffensive great-grandson Louis XVI, who suffered for Louis XIV's sins. The Pyramids are masterpieces of architectural skill and of organized co-operative work, but surely this skill and organization would have been better employed on building barrages and digging canals or drains. The British playwright Bernard Shaw is said to have made this remark when he saw the Pyramids. Some Ancient Egyptian poems about a social revolution have been discovered and interpreted. This was the earliest social revolution that we know of; it brought to an end the age of the Pyramid-builders. The writers of these poems deplore the fact that everything has been turned upside down; that the mighty have been put down from their seat and that the humble and meek have been exalted; but, when I read these poems, I have a feeling of exhilaration. I feel that this was a just retribution for what had been a most flagrant social injustice.

Is not the space programme as offensive morally in its present high priority as the building of the Pyramids and the building of the Palace at Versailles? I feel that the space programme is morally indefensible, not in itself, but because it has been given priority over the feeding and clothing and housing of the poor majority of the human race. I feel that this crying need ought to have the first call on mankind's resources, energy, and skill. Also, I suspect that the governments of the United States and the Soviet Union would not have spent on this space programme the enormous resources that they have actually spent on it if they had not been competing with each other for political and military ascendancy on this planet. I consider that this competition is childish in itself, is immoral in an age in which the majority of mankind is poor, and is criminal in an age in which the competing great powers are armed with the atomic weapon. For these reasons, if I were to find myself in the position of being a world dictator invested with irresistible power—of which, fortunately, there is no likelihood—I would immediately put a stop to all present space programmes. I would not delete these from my agenda, but I would give them a very low place in the order of my priorities.

I think that the value for mankind of the exploration of outer space cannot yet be discerned. What are we going to find in outer space? In exploring the surface of this planet the West Europeans once found a North and a South America. Later on, we found an Antarctic Continent. This is one of the larger continents; if I am right, it is at least as big as Australia, if not bigger. But it has not been of much use to us so far. We may find some use for it; there may be marvellous deposits of minerals buried under its snow and ice, and we might be able to melt the ice-cap by using nuclear power.

My point is that the difference in value between the Americas and the South Polar Continent is relevant to the exploration of outer space and to the value, for us, of the planets which we are perhaps going to reach in other solar systems within our own galaxy or in other galaxies. Is what we are going to meet with in outer space going to be just another Antarctic Continent, or is it going to be another North and South America, which would give mankind a larger usable habitat? We do not know. What I would say is: we have plenty of time; so let us postpone the space programme until we have raised the poor majority of the human race on the face of this planet to the level of the rich minority. Then we could resume the space programme with good consciences and with a moral right to indulge in this new adventure.

I have already discussed at some length the likelihood, as it seems to me, that an atomic war—which might mean the end of man's history on this planet and which would in any case be a calamity that might well reduce mankind again to the pre-civilizational level—can only be avoided by the establishment of a world government, and I have said that the lessons of history seem to show that, in the present state of the World, a world government would probably take a highly tyrannical, dictatorial form.

I want to see a world government established, and, in spite of the formidable difficulties in the way, I think it is not impossible that it might be brought into existence by mutual agreement and not by the imposition of dictatorial rule on the majority of man-

kind by a minority which held the power conferred by technological 'know-how' and which, for its own selfish reasons, was
determined to maintain 'law and order' at the expense of the
masses.

Today the human race has become virtually a single family. To
a certain extent the fusion or unification of the civilizations of the
East and the West has already taken place. The technological
inventions of the last five centuries, multiplying and becoming
more efficient at an accelerating pace, have knit together the whole
of the habitable and traversable surface of this planet for good or
for evil. Man's habitat on this planet has been reduced, in terms of
the time taken to communicate and of the facilities for communication, to the dimensions of a Neolithic village. It takes
almost as little time today to get about the World as it did in the
Neolithic Age to get from the centre of the village to the furthest
of the village's fields. This is not an exaggeration. So now we
ought to be able all to live together as one family. In these unprecedented circumstances, the continuation of disunity is surely a
senseless and dangerous anachronism.

We cannot live together as a single family—live under one roof,
so to speak—unless we have in common a minimum of manners
and customs, ideas and ideals. Technology provides us with the
physical means of arriving at a common way of life, but it cannot
supply ideas and ideals. Can mankind unify itself politically and
economically without at the same time unifying itself in its religion
and its ideology? It is well known that political federation cannot
be workable or durable if there are serious differences in the ethical
standards and outlooks of the different component members. For
instance, the United States had to be reunited at the cost of a civil
war because slavery had been a legalized institution in some states,
while it had been made illegal in other states. The United States
could not remain half slave and half free.

Uniformity of ethical standards and ideals is certainly a necessary
enabling condition for unity of any kind. Is ethical uniformity
compatible with variety in ideology and religion? I believe that it
is compatible, and I believe that religious and ideological variety are
good things in themselves, because they correspond to the variety

of human nature and meet its needs. I have already made this point in answering the questions about religion. However, I think that, now that the World has been unified on the technological plane, religious and ideological variety will no longer be compatible with the survival of mankind if it is still accompanied, as it has been in the past and unfortunately still is today, by animosity, rivalry, competition for dominance, and conflict.

I hope that ideologies and religions will cease to be part of the local cultural heritage. I should like all of them to be included in every child's heritage all over the world. I know that children want definite answers: Yes or No? Black or White? Is Christianity or is Islam right? Is Buddhism or is Judaism right? Is Communism or is Capitalism right? Children do not like to be told that there are alternative possibilities; that there is a bit of right in one and a bit in the other, and that we have to take account of both. But surely it is a necessary part of a child's education to know that things are not really clear-cut and are not either pure black or pure white. I think this is the best preparation that a child can have for entering into a life in which people of many different cultures are coming together into a single family. So I should like children all over the World to learn about all of the World's historic religions and about the different ideologies, so that individual choices in the matter of religion and ideology can be made by everyone in due course, at an age when the individual is mature enough to know his or her own mind as an adult person. I should like to see the confrontation between religions and ideologies become an opportunity and a stimulus for choice, instead of continuing to be an automatic cause of irrational hostility and strife.

Consider Communism and Capitalism. Capitalism protects individual freedom at the expense of social justice; Communism puts social justice before freedom. But both justice and freedom are indispensable; there has to be a compromise between them; and there are many possible different choices of the line at which the compromise should be drawn. In Communist and Capitalist society alike, there is both a private sector and a public sector of the economy. At present, the line between these two sectors is drawn at a different point in the two régimes. In Communism the public sector is given the larger share; in Capitalism the private sector is predominant. However, both Communism and Capitalism are being re-moulded under the pressure of one and the same irresistible force, namely modern technology. I expect to see the dividing-line between the public sector and the private sector in both Communism and Capitalism shift till, in both régimes, this dividing-line arrives at the same point. When this happens, Communism and Capitalism will have become identical with each other in fact, even if they continue to wear their present different labels.

This convergence between Communism and Capitalism is to be expected, I think, because Communists and Capitalists are confronted by an identical common problem that overrides the difference between their outlooks. Both need to discover how to make life tolerable in the new man-made artificial environment that we have substituted for our natural environment. The problems of urbanism, pollution, psychological disorientation, and outbreaks of irrational violence are common to all mankind today, and these problems transcend the traditional differences between ideologies.

In setting out to promote the unity of mankind, I believe that our goal ought to be to lead a double life, at one level as citizens of the World and at another level as members of a community small enough to make it possible for the relations between its members to be personal.

I have suggested already that, in order to make the coming world city tolerable, we ought to articulate it into what I call 'wards', within which each inmate would be able to know all the other inmates personally, and would be able to meet them without the need for using mechanized wheels. But, now that technology has annihilated distance, there can be other communities of this small neighbourly size whose members can be scattered all over the World.

Some such communities exist already. The present handful of tip-top mathematicians and physicists already constitutes a world-wide community of brothers. I have been four times to the Institute for Advanced Study at Princeton, New Jersey, in the United States, which is one of the World's centres for advanced mathematical physics, and I have seen physicists meeting each other there personally for the first time. I have seen them greeting each other just like brothers. They had felt lonely, because they speak a language which no one round them could understand. So, they found it thrilling to meet in the flesh some of the few other people who can speak the same language. They are a very small community, but they are scattered all over the World: in America, in Europe, in India, in Eastern Asia, everywhere.

The musicians, doctors, artists, and scholars are more numerous than the mathematicians and the physicists, but they, too, could establish a family relation among themselves by articulating themselves into hierarchies of groups and sub-groups. My wife and I were once in Philadelphia, and a friend of ours who is a musician, an American of Russian origin, introduced us to other musicians in Philadelphia. They were of different national origins but I could see that they were a band of brothers. Differences of origin and of cultural background counted for nothing compared to their common passion for music. A few years later, when I was in California, I met the Philadelphia Orchestra coming back from Japan, where they had had enthusiastic audiences. It is remarkable that, in Japan, Western music now has a numerous public. Music gets over the barriers of language, as I have already noted. Japanese music is very different in style from Western music; it is more like Turkish or Indian or Arab music; but, since music is a non-linguistic medium of communication, it is possible to understand and appreciate the same kind of music all over the World. I think that music and musicians are going to be great unifiers of mankind.

Here our technological means of communication can be made to play a humanizing role. Technology has now made it possible for diasporas, 'dispersions'—a word taken from the dispersed Jewish community all over the World—to establish a community life which can be as close and as genuine as the companionship among the members of local communities. I look forward to a time when every human being will belong to three societies. He will be a member of the world society, a citizen of the world state; he will be a member of one of the local 'wards' of the world city, a local community in which every inmate will know every other; and, in the third place, he will be a member of a world-wide diaspora, and this, too, will consist of small enough numbers of people for them to be in personal relations with each other. They may frequently meet face to face, but, if they do not, they will be able to communicate constantly by letters or by telephone, and they may be able to see each other's faces on a television screen. They will, in fact, be in personal contact, though they will be scattered all over the face of the globe.

In my expectation, this network of diasporas—the physicists, the mathematicians, the musicians, the doctors, the artists, and so on—is one of the new 'configurations' of social life that are going to link the whole World together.

Another question that we must consider is whether regional integration—for example the European Common Market—is likely to help or to hinder the establishment of a world government? Under present-day technological conditions, any integration on any scale has to be political as well as economic. Indeed, as early as the nineteenth century, the German Zollverein (Customs' Union) needed to be supplemented by the creation of the Second German Reich. The Zollverein is historically significant in so far as it proved to have been an effective preparation for the creation of the Second German Empire. The European Economic Community, which is the most important present experiment in regional integration, will have likewise to integrate politically as well as economically if it is to come to something.

A federal state would perhaps be likely to function more smoothly if its component units were approximately uniform in their scale; and, if that were true, the establishment in Western Europe of a regional unit of the same calibre as the United States and the Soviet Union might be propitious for the establishment of a federal world state. However, the histories of the United States and Switzerland show that a uniformity in the scale of the component states is not an indispensable condition for the success of a federal state. The crucial requirement is not that; it is the establishment of a direct relation between the individual citizen and the federal government, above the heads of the state governments. In both the United States and Switzerland the states members differ very greatly in their scale. But, contrary to the fears of the smaller American states at the time when the United States Constitution was being drafted, this disparity in the size of the constituent states has not been a cause of instability, or a threat of disintegration, either for the United States or for Switzerland. In the nineteenth century, each of those two federal states had a civil war. In Switzerland there was the war of the so-called Sonderbund, a secessionist federation, and in the United States there was the famous civil war between the Union and the abortive Southern Confederacy. But the cause of the civil war was not, in either case, the tension between big members of the Confederation and small members. In the United States the cause was slavery; in Switzerland the cause was partly a difference of religion and partly a political difference between conservatives and radicals.

On the other hand, a regional super-power, such as the United States and the Soviet Union are already and as the European Economic Community might become, might perhaps be misled more easily than a midget state—say Luxemburg or Guatemala—into falling into the illusion that it could continue to stand alone, as a fully sovereign independent state, in spite of the progressive increase in the scale of human operations of all kinds that is being produced by the progress of technology.

If the present 140 or so local sovereign independent states on the surface of this planet were to coagulate into six or twelve super-powers, it might prove to be more difficult to induce these six super-powers to take the further step of federating into a world state than it would be to induce the present local states to do this. I will give you a striking example. The constitution of the Ancient Greek federal state known as the Achaean Confederation was one of the constitutions that was studied by the Founding Fathers of the American Union. One of the foremost of the Achaean states-men who lived in the third and second century B.C., Philopoemen, was a citizen of Megalopolis. Megalopolis seems a small city-state now, but, as the name shows, it was a very large city-state for Ancient Greece. Philopoemen took every opportunity of breaking up the larger members of the Achaean Confederation, including his own home state Megalopolis, and of giving separate direct membership to the splinter states that he had detached.

Notice that, at the beginning of the North American civil war, the Union Government did the same. It broke up the state of Virginia, which was a large state, into Virginia and West Virginia. West Virginia was Unionist and the rest of Virginia was Secessionist. The Federal Government eagerly accepted West Virginia as a separate state, because this diminished the excessive power of Virginia in the Union.

I expect that, before a world state is achieved, some additional regional integrations will have been established. I think the E.E.C. is now virtually certain of continuing to exist, whether it expands beyond the Six or not. I think there are likely to be partial, though perhaps not comprehensive, unions of the Spanish-American states and of the Arab states. Both of these two possibilities seem at present rather remote, notwithstanding the pressure of the United States on Latin America and of Israel on the Arab world. On the other hand, there are some rich and highly-civilized small states which might hesitate less to become separate members of a world federal state than to enter into a regional federation. I am thinking here of Switzerland, Sweden, the Lebanese Republic, Singapore, and possibly also Hong Kong and Taiwan. I therefore expect that a future world state will be composed, like Switzerland and the United States and the Soviet Union, of constituent states that will differ from each other greatly in scale.

Let us now go on to consider some of the principal difficulties that will have to be overcome before human beings can become members of a single family. One of the most obvious of these difficulties is that of the large number of different languages which are spoken in different parts of the world. I have dealt with this obstacle already in discussing education, and I need only repeat here that I think that the only solution is for people everywhere to become polyglot. Learning to speak, read, and write at least one foreign language ought to be given a very high priority in education all over the World. Then there is the question of racial feeling. Anthropologists tell us that there are not really any 'pure races'. Even in the most remote and segregated regions a mixture of races is to be found. But racial feeling undoubtedly exists and is something about which we are all concerned. It is a danger to the World, and most of us are ashamed of it. Dogs do not feel racial feeling against each other. A black dog and a white dog will play together; each of them knows that they are both dogs. But unfortunately a black human being and a white human being, except when they are children, sometimes feel hostility towards each other, and, among people who do have race feeling, this feeling is strong, and it quickly expresses itself in violence.

Fortunately, some people are free from race feeling. For instance, in Western Pakistan, where I have travelled, there are now people of many races, ranging from the darkest to the lightest coloured skins; yet they seem to me to be quite unconscious of their physical racial differences. Some of them have come there as refugees from India, because they share the Muslim religion with the people who were living there already. The bond of their common religion overcomes any consciousness of difference of race.

Or look at Latin America. In Brazil there are quite a large number—I think half a million—of Japanese settlers. They and the Brazilians of Portuguese origin mix with each other and intermarry with each other, apparently without any feeling on either side of antipathy because of race.

In Mexico, about 85 per cent of the people are of mixed race. Their blood is mainly native pre-Columbian American; the rest is partly European, partly Negro. The Mexicans, too, are quite unconscious of racial differences. You will find people of almost completely white race far down the social ladder, and people who are almost completely American-Indian by race right up at the top. If you want to understand Mexico, you should go to the shrine of the Virgin of Guadalupe, who is the patron goddess of Mexico. According to the legend, the Virgin Mary appeared to a Mexican-Indian convert to Christianity as an Indian goddess with an Indian skin and in Indian dress; she performed miracles which the Roman Catholic ecclesiastical authorities eventually accepted as being authentic; and she became the common patron of both the conquering Spaniards and the conquered Mexicans.

Even in the United States there is one state, Hawaii, where

people seem to be free from racial feeling. In Hawaii you will find Japanese, Chinese, Portuguese, Polynesians, and Americans all mixing with each other and inter-marrying with each other— apparently quite happily.

These examples show that race feeling is not implanted in human beings by nature. So-called racial differences are literally only skin-deep, and they are, I think, of no real importance, considering that man's distinctive feature is his spirit and not his physique. I do not think that in Japan there is any race feeling between the Japanese and the Ainu; as far as there is a difference, it is a cultural one. The Japanese are culturally advanced, whereas the Ainu, who belong physically to the same race, more or less, as the North Europeans, are culturally backward. I think it is true everywhere that it is the cultural, not the racial, difference that is important.

The worst racialists are the so-called Nordics, that is the North European peoples and their settlers overseas in the Americas and Australia; the high-class Hindus; and the Jews. It is a mystery why some peoples should have this racial feeling and others not. Fortunately, the peoples who have a strong racial prejudice are in a minority, and, since some peoples are immune to racial antagonism, it is evident that the peoples who do have racial feeling could overcome it in themselves if they chose. In Britain it is disconcerting for us to find that, the moment a relatively small number of Pakistanis and West Indians have settled here, the native white majority at once starts to behave like the Whites in the United States. In Britain we used to be rather proud of being free from race feeling. Now that we know that we have it, it is our business to cure ourselves of it.

I think that race feeling is a menace to world peace and an obstacle to the unity of mankind, but I do not despair of seeing the rest of the World go the Mexican, Pakistani, and Hawaiian way and become oblivious of physical racial differences.

I have said that I believe that differences of culture play a much more important part in race feeling than differences in the colour of the skin or other varieties in physical appearance. I think that cultural pluralism through education is the solution of the problem of cultural differences, as it is of the problem of differences of language. East Asians—Japanese, Koreans, Vietnamese, and the other peoples of Indo-China—have at least three cultures. Besides their own local culture, they have Chinese culture in some form and Indian culture in the form of Buddhism. In the Christian and Muslim part of the World, culture consists of two strands: one is Jewish and the other is Graeco-Roman. These two strands are to some extent in a state of tension with each other, but they supplement each other fruitfully. The existing cultures are, in fact, all syncretisms. I think we might develop a world culture which selected the best out of the regional cultures and made it a common possession for the whole human race.

One manifestation of a difference in cultural background that is apt to cause friction and prejudice is the difference in the social customs and habits of people who become neighbours. It is certainly very difficult when communities that have been previously segregated from each other, so that their social customs have grown far apart, are suddenly intermingled at close quarters in big cities. This is one of the difficulties in the way of the assimilation of the Southern Negroes in the United States when they move to Northern cities, and of the coloured immigrants in Great Britain, and it exists even where they share a common language with the people among whom they are trying to settle. In a crowded city where the newcomers are more noisy and talkative than their old-established neighbours, it is hard for them to live close together without friction. But the difficulty may be only temporary if the two parties can learn to show consideration for each other and to modify their respective customs in order to accommodate themselves to each other. Certainly, the success of mixed marriages in places such as Hawaii shows that this social obstacle can be overcome even in the most intimate of all relationships.

In fact, though some of the obstacles which hinder the attainment of world unity are obviously serious, I do not myself think that any of them are insurmountable.

One last question that arises when we are considering the possibility that a world state could be established by mutual agreement and not by force is whether the United Nations, as this institution exists today, could be the embryo of a world government.

The United Nations has already developed, on a world-wide scale, two of the organs that a state of any dimensions requires, namely a representative legislature and an efficient, devoted, and honest civil service which has an *esprit de corps*. However, the United Nations legislature is defective. It consists of the Assembly and the Security Council (the Security Council is both Senate and Executive). When compared with the constitution of the United States, the United Nations legislature corresponds to the United States Senate only. There is not yet any world-wide representative assembly that corresponds to the House of Representatives in Washington, D.C., which represents the individual citizens of the United States. As I have already said, the experience of all attempts to create and maintain states with federal constitutions seems to show that a direct relationship between the federal government and individual citizens is essential for the success of such attempts.

Other serious lacks in the present constitution of the United Nations, regarded as a possible embryo of the future world state, are the weakness of its executive organs and the inadequacy of its financial resources. The executive power of the United Nations is no greater than the authority that its states members choose to allow it to exercise. The Security Council, with its officer, the Secretary General, serves to some extent as an executive organ of the United Nations, but the Security Council can be, and frequently has been, defied with impunity, not only by the superpowers who have the right of veto, but also by small and weak states-members.

Even when the Security Council has been able to come to a unanimous decision about how to deal with some particular problem, it is hard for it to enforce the decision itself in the absence of a permanent international police force. A police force is necessary on an international scale as well as in the domestic constitution of local states. We human beings are irrational and turbulent; some of us are criminal; we need government, and government needs to have physical force at its command for asserting its authority in the last resort. So far, the United Nations has raised international police forces only to meet temporary emergencies here and there —for instance, in the Congo and in the Middle East. The United

Nations has appealed to states that are non-great-powers to volunteer to provide contingents, and its appeals have met with a fairly good response. I have seen an international peace-keeping force at work on the Arab side of the frontier in the Gaza Strip. I was impressed by the effectiveness of the co-operation between contingents supplied by many different countries. But I should prefer to see a permanent international police force composed of international personnel, trained and controlled and paid by the United Nations itself.

Here, however, the financial weakness of the United Nations under its present constitution comes into play. For its revenue, the United Nations is dependent on the contributions of the states-members, and they are able to withhold their contributions, temporarily at least, if they disapprove of some line of action on which the Security Council has decided against their wishes. If the United States Government in Washington had no taxing power of its own and had to beg from the governments of the States, it would obtain very little revenue.

I think, therefore, that the United Nations will need strengthening in a number of ways if it is ever to develop into a true world government.

7

Hopes and Expectations for the Younger Generation

WAKAIZUMI: Professor Toynbee, we have ranged very widely in our discussions and have touched on many issues. May we move finally into a more personal, a more intimate area of concern? May I ask you to talk to us about your thoughts on the future of the younger generation? Having had more than eighty years' experience of life by now, as you have, what advice do you think of offering to the younger generation of today? What do you expect of them? What do you hope for them?

TOYNBEE: What is my advice to the younger generation now that I myself am eighty-two years old? Well, my first advice to you is to keep the spirit of youth until you are dead. So often young people have grown up, thinking: 'We will be different from our parents' generation. We won't become stiff and conservative-minded and intolerant and conformist. We will always keep our youthful ideals.' And then, as they get older, age gets the better of them and they become middle-aged; they become just what they objected to in the people of their parents' generation. Now, your generation is in a very special position. You happen to be living at a turning-point in the history of the human race. You have a great opportunity, and you will not be able to use this opportunity unless you do succeed in retaining, all through life, the spirit of youth—that is, the spirit of generosity, of readiness for change, of idealism, of disinterestedness. Try, I would say above all, to remain compassionate-minded and generous-minded; try to remain capable of entering into other people's states of mind and of sympathizing with them even when you strongly disagree with them. Try to put yourselves in the other people's place and to see why they hold these opinions or do these things with which you so strongly disagree. Go on opposing the conservative-minded members of your parents' generation. Certainly try to resist them and to defeat them in as far as their ideas and ideals seem to you to be mistaken, but do this in the Gandhi spirit; do it without hatred.

When the Mahatma Gandhi was leading the Indian people in their movement to get rid of British rule, whenever his followers began to have strong feelings of hostility towards the British, he would always say: 'Stop until you have got over this feeling of hostility. We won't go on till you have. It is only when you cease to hate the British that we can afford to go on opposing them.' And he consistently kept the temper down, so that, in the end, the Indians did get rid of British rule without any lasting hostility between the British and the Indians, thanks to Gandhi's spirit.

That spirit is the spirit that we should all of us—young and old —try to live up to. In other words, try to make your love prevail over your feelings of hostility, and then try not to become defensive-minded and repressive yourselves as you slide into middle age. And do not let yourselves be discouraged or embittered by the smallness of the success that you are likely to achieve in trying to make life better. You certainly will not be able, in a single generation, to create an earthly paradise. Who could expect that? But, if you make life ever so little better, you will have done splendidly, and your lives will have been worth while. Remember what I have said before about the load of *karma*. Every generation in turn, including your generation and your parents' generation and your still unborn children's generation, is handicapped by the *karma* that has been accumulating since life on this planet began. But just as *karma* can accumulate, so it can be dissipated. The load can be diminished and can finally be thrown off, by good action undoing the effects of bad action. That is the Buddha's teaching, and I believe it is the truth.

Your generation will find itself handicapped in its turn. It would be childish to expect to be released from *karma* by some miracle. No human being in any generation can expect that. But, as I say, you can release yourselves from *karma* partially, and the best way of doing this is by developing, by whatever means are open to you, the spirit which inspires self-sacrificing love.

Now I have a practical suggestion to put to you. I have said that, in my view, two obvious possible alternatives confront the human race today, and both seem to me to be bad. One is self-liquidation by an atomic war. The other—which would certainly be the lesser of the two evils—is avoidance of war through a unification of the World under a dictatorial world régime in which the rich and powerful minority would league together, all over the World, to hold down the poor and backward majority.

The avoidance of atomic war would be the lesser evil, but the establishment of a dictatorial type of world government would also be a very great evil. Here is a challenge for you of the younger generation. Can you find a middle way between a war which might end in the destruction of the whole human race—or at any rate of a large part of it in the more developed, more highly civilized regions of the World—and a repressive world government? Can you find some form of world unity that will enable the human race to survive and prosper without oppression and without reaction?

I do think that it is within your power to take the first steps in this direction. I will repeat here a point which I have made earlier. When you are protesting—especially when your protests are justified and when the middle-aged people who have power in their hands at the moment do not take you seriously and laugh at you or get angry with you—it is very tempting to make sure of attracting their attention by taking to violence. But violence inevitably provokes a 'backlash'. If you young people resort to violence, then the people in power will use counter-violence, and they are likely to be better armed and better organized than you can be. If demonstrating students throw stones or grenades or bombs or arm themselves with whatever other weapons are available to them, the riot police and the national guard will have more, and more deadly, weapons with which they will be able to repress you. Then there may be civil war, and the forces of reaction are likely to be the victors. The maintenance of 'law and order' will then be given priority over the redressing of the evils to which you are drawing attention, and in the end we shall have a fascist world state. So, above all, try to be patient and avoid violence. Take your lessons from the leaders of the great philosophies and religions. Try to copy the gentleness, the patience, the long-suffering of the Buddha and Jesus and of other great souls, such as Gandhi, who have appeared among us in our own time.

Closing Remarks

WAKAIZUMI: Professor Toynbee, we have travelled a long way in this comprehensive discussion. We have probed back into the past in the light of your extensive knowledge, and we have ventured into the uncertain realms of the future. I hope that our readers will share the sense of urgency that both you and I feel, that man must determine his own destiny through a retrieval of values that are truly humane. At the end of their passage through today's troubled world, I hope they can be as tranquil as you, and can be equally ready to entrust the safety and welfare of future generations of humanity to their successors. I hope you will live for many years yet and that you will see some of the changes that we both hope for come into being.

We have seen how today man balances precariously on a tight-rope between optimism and pessimism, between good and evil, between rationality and blind emotion, between the threat of annihilation and the hope of peace, between the ideal and the real, between the past and the future. We could easily fall from our precarious position into the abyss of self-destruction.

Nevertheless, your interpretation of the lessons of history seems to be that man has, so far, been able to overcome the difficulties with which he has been faced and has been able to find social and philosophical solutions to the problems created by the advance of technology. If this has been so in the past, why should it not also be possible in the future?

The changes that we hope for lie in a re-structured code of living, in a more humane attitude to life, and in a renewal of compassion and love. Perhaps if man can feel this love for all living beings, he may succeed in surviving the future. Through these advances in the concern of man for all his fellow creatures, we also hope for a return to a more thoughtful approach to man's problems and to a rejection of destructive impulses.

We have faced many contemporary fears—of a third world war, of the retreat from reason and the collapse of established institutions, of man finding himself at the mercy of his machines and losing his sense of direction amidst a welter of suffocating knowledge and of overwhelming social change. We have faced the possibility of the gap between the rich and poor nations increasing to a point at which there might be a violent resolution of forces. We have looked at the various ways in which the young people in both rich and poor societies express their hopes and needs. We have looked at man as being egoistic, possessive, nationalistic, alienated from himself and from his human environment.

Yet we have done all this with a positive belief in the vital spiritual and compassionate nature of man. We have envisaged the possibility that he can control technological progress, that he can work towards a peaceful world, that through educational effort he can arrive at a better understanding of his human condition and can find a new meaning for his destiny. You have emphasized the task embedded in the very nature of man: to love, to understand, and to create.

As always, it is the young towards whom humanity turns for the insurance of its future, and we have not lost faith in them.

Thank you, Professor Toynbee, for allowing me to accompany you on this journey of exploration. We have not found a new world in our few days together, but perhaps we can say that we have at least seen a glimpse of the road towards it. It is your long vision that has seen it most clearly, and I hope that, through this volume, others may also be able to perceive it.

Index